NAMMA BANGALORE 2.0

Shoba Narayan is the author of seven books. She has been a journalist and columnist for 30 years, writing about travel, food, wine, culture, crafts and relationships, for national and international publications. She has won a James Beard Award and a Pulitzer Fellowship. She has taught and lectured at universities in India and abroad.

She is interested in Indian aesthetics, and has researched its influence on jewellery, music, textiles and scents. She founded and co-created a website called *Project LooM*, which documents the weaving traditions of India. She is a birdwatcher, wine-drinker and gadget geek. Her lifelong mission is to get fit without exercising and lose weight without dieting.

NAMMA BANGALORE 2.0

CULTURE, CODING, CUISINE, CREATIVITY

SHOBA NARAYAN

RUPA

Published by
Rupa Publications India Pvt. Ltd 2025
161-B/4, Gulmohar House,
Yusuf Sarai Community Centre,
New Delhi 110049

Sales centres:
Bengaluru Chennai
Hyderabad Kolkata Mumbai

Some parts of this book were first published by HT Media and Condé Nast.

P-ISBN: 978-93-7003-182-1
E-ISBN: 978-93-7003-775-5

First impression 2025

10 9 8 7 6 5 4 3 2 1

Printed in India

Dedicated to
Rohini
Bengaluru's wildlife-whisperer who hugs trees, nourishes streams, summons falcons, turtles and other wondrous creatures, including humans.

Contents

ARTS AND CULTURE

SUBCULTURES AND IDENTITY

EVERYDAY LIFE AND INTROSPECTION

Introduction

Every now and then, my friends want to move to Bangalore. They are attracted by its weather and vibrant tech scene. Since I write books and articles about this city, they often ask for advice of various sorts: good schools, cost of living, and most often, where to live. For the last question, I have a stock answer. I describe various neighbourhoods in Bangalore and then offer my final tip: live near a bazaar. Unless you are the kind who doesn't like bazaars, in which case my advice would be the opposite: live in a gated community.

Cities claim your heart in many ways. Some are flamboyant and classy, with many world-class museums, buildings and performing arts venues. Others play up their age with ancient alleys and historical landmarks. Some cities, though, try to walk the fine line between doing all of the above. Bangalore is one of those cities. The region it stands on is objectively one of the oldest, not just in India but on earth. Bangalore stands atop a Precambrian geologic rock formation that was formed roughly 4.3 billion years ago. Lalbagh rock, that all of us clamber upon, is part of this geologic time. When you stand on top of it, you are touching one of the oldest parts of earth. Bangalore city, on the other hand, is layered. It does not have the historical heft of neighbouring Chennai with its Chola kings and colonial remnants. It does not have Mughal history and grand buildings like Delhi. It is not as vibrant in its performing arts venues as Mumbai. It does not have the colonial buildings of Kolkata. Bangalore is a bit of a khichdi—with all of the above and none of the above.

So, what makes Bangalore unique? Well, for one, its weather. The second anomaly is that it is not near a river, which most global cities need in order to set up their civilizations. Bangalore became a settlement because it was at the crossroads of the North–South East–West trade routes. Today, this city has been overtaken by technology, first with IT and now with its startup culture. If you want to see Bangalore before it became synonymous with software, you have to go to its bazaars. It is where all the wheeling and dealing happens.

On nearly every weekday morning, I have a routine. I wear a simple cotton saree and walk to Russell Market. I may not necessarily enter the market, but all along the way are vendors who I know and have cultivated over the many years that I have lived in Bangalore. There is the dour vendor on Dharmaraja Koil street who only sells banana leaves, a lady who sells greens and knows their medicinal properties, a flower guy who can custom-make arrangements for parties as long as they are Indian-style garland-type ones. I chat with them, haggle for vegetables, and learn new things.

To see the city that you live in as a spectacle, an object

of visual interest and social interaction, requires that you be a flaneur: that old French word which connotes loitering without a purpose. There are several cities in the world that lend themselves to this sort of approach to life in the city. Most European cities, for instance, let your wander. In India, this is difficult largely because of the trifecta of heat, traffic and pollution. In Bangalore, though, this is possible, particularly if you live in densely populated areas like mine. Shivaji Nagar is full of narrow alleys and lanes that connote a time before vehicles.

The trick is to choose unchanging eternal sights—that are not linked to any event or season—as your touchstones. In my area, this means choosing old temples to goddesses like Muthyalamma, Angala Parameshwari and Mariamma. It means the St. Mary's Church and the Juma Masjid. It means the old attar sellers who have populated the place forever. And of course Russell Market, where a rotating cast of garland makers, butchers and vegetable vendors ply their trade.

With that said, I want to give you specific instances of how to walk through your neighbourhood with a flaneur's approach.

Look for cobblers and tailors as you walk. Stop for a moment to peer into their shops. Some will have boots and buttons, some will have men sitting on the floor and doing intricate embroidery. Punjab tailors or LB Prakash in Commercial Street, for instance, are where I go to get intricate work done. You can squat on the ground next to the sequin guy or the embroiderer and discuss French knots and roses with them. Isn't that luxury?

Look for gully cricket. Still happens in small lanes all

over Bangalore. If you are in the mood and have time, join in. It is a great way to know the neighbourhood.

Look at street names. In Shivaji Nagar for instance, there is a Fruit Street, Murphy Road, and Ashur Khanna Street. I wonder about these names and these people. Who were they and how did they influence Bangalore?

In that question lies a new exploration. Being curious about your neighbourhood lets you peel open the layers that are hidden in plain sight. They let you both be a tourist in your own city and also get to know the place that you call home a little better. But for all this, the necessary but not sufficient condition is that you must walk.

Preface

How to read this book

This is my second book about Namma Bangalore. While this book is nominally divided into sections and chapters, really it is a set of musings about the city that I have called home for the last 20 years.

So pick a section. Open a page. Read. Repeat.

Food and Drink

Dating and dosas: Being single in Bangalore

Has lack of qualification ever stopped Indians from volunteering opinions? No, right?

I say this as preamble for this column where I, a married woman, talk about the single life in Bangalore. By some estimates, I am overqualified, having been in a stable relationship for several decades. To be fair, I interviewed a ton of single folks before writing this. Some threads emerged.

Dating isn't set up for introverts. Whether you are on Bumble or any other dating app, whether you attend singles meetups that happen regularly in the city, the whole set-up favours extroverts who project confidence. So what do you do if you are not much of a talker?

'Action' was the answer given to me. If you are not good at the self-marketing that needs to happen when you do speed-dating, consider just speed. Join one of the running clubs in Bangalore. They meet on weekends in Cubbon Park and run together. Folks are friendly, inclusive, interesting and best of all, don't force you to talk.

You can just show up, stretch a bit, sip water, make eye-contact with folks you find interesting, and then run in the group. Over time, that cute single you are interested in will come up to you with a simple 'Good run, wasn't it?', and off you go.

The same applies to the many hiking groups that exist in the city. India Hikes, the portal, offers overnight hiking trips to Savanadurga, Rangaswamy Betta, Nandi Hills and other excellent hiking spots. Talking isn't necessary, walking is.

Nature is the other area where folks aren't judged by how much they talk. As a bird-watcher, I can tell you that nature allows for singles and silence. When you are standing in Lalbagh and watching a green sandpiper (a shorebird) on the lake, there is no need to speak and impress. You can stand next to the object of your interest and ask a simple question: 'Do you know the name of that bird?' A non-profit website called Bngbirds announces bird-watching meetups that happen every Sunday in different parts of the city. Carry a pair of binoculars and go.

Dating is both exhilarating and exhausting. There is the hope of course, that you will meet THE ONE, which, I can tell you is a fool's errand. The problem with the whole 'soulmate' idea is that it forces you to imagine one person to be attentive friend, red-hot lover, caregiving parent, and fun-filled date at the same time. It is as if you have rolled up all your needs into one person, rather than parsing it out to different people—which is what happens in real life. That's a lot of pressure on any person. No wonder things fall apart.

Clubs like Let's Socialise and Small World which

organize singles meetups make the whole dating thing a caricature. The hired facilitator forces you to do uncomfortable things like salsa dancing and clay-painting. Tell me, in all the relationships that you have seen (whether it is parent, sibling, cousin or friend), have you ever once heard a couple talk about salsa-dancing as a way to improve the relationship? Clay-painting at least forces you to get your hands dirty, quite literally. It takes away from the tension of being well-dressed because guess what, you are going to have soil on your clothes anyhow.

Speed-dating is a different beast and rather exhausting. Going in with low expectations and having a sense of humour helps defray the tension, I am told, but most singles hate speed-dating. They do it because they work at start-ups with little free time and believe that speed-dating can be an 'efficient' way to meet a future partner. Having a pre-prepared script or at least a few bullet points about what you are going to talk about helps. Asking normal questions (Where do you work?), personal ones (I love going on safaris. Do you?), and standout questions (Did you like where you grew up? When was the last time you were afraid?) help you stay memorable in the minds of all those folks you meet for three to five minutes.

Bookstores are a good place to meet folks if you happen to like to read. A couple of weeks ago, at Atta Galatta, I came upon a stack of gift-wrapped books by the counter. When I asked Subodh Shankar, the genial owner of the bookstore, about them, he said, 'Oh, those are what we call a "blind date with a book", in that you don't know what book you are getting.'

There are a lot of dates happening this month in

Bangalore, with Valentine's Day around the corner. When I went on Tinder's section on dating ideas in Bangalore, it recommended Cubbon Park, Lalbagh, Wonderla, and weirdly, the ISKCON temple as places to go to find single folks. Actually, maybe the temple, church, gurudwara or mosque is not a far-fetched idea at all. It happens even today all over India. When I asked two young women, who work as nurses in my building, about how youngsters of marriageable age meet in Chikmagalur or Sakleshpur, they said, 'At family weddings or in temples.'

So go ahead and date away. Do it your way, whether it is through a jog in the park, a drink at a bar, or dinner and a movie.

∞

Benne dosa and buzz: A breakfast walk through Basavanagudi

India has a masala dosa problem. This folded potato-filled, fermented-rice, flat circular piece of deliciousness has overtaken the world. The problem is that equally good variations of this form get lost in the focus on this one type of dosa. So go ahead and have your Mysore masala dosa, but please also spare a thought for other kinds of dosas. Consider, for example, the khali dosa. This was how it was described: 'A pillowy soft dosa that melts in your mouth. You will be amazed by the deliciousness, especially since they use no oil in their preparation.'

The writer of these words was Nishanth Shamanna, who graduated with an MBA from Stanford this year. He was leading a group of Stanford alums on a breakfast walk through Basavanagudi. I was the interloper who joined them, just for the food.

We began at Hotel Dwarka, iconic in South Bangalore. We Indians still continue to call small restaurants 'hotels', probably because it is easier on the tongue. Over 50 years old, Hotel Dwarka is famous for many things including its masala dosa. Our group, however, opted for the khali dosa, which was indeed fluffy. Two soft dosas with 'aloo palya' on the side, some butter on top and liberal amounts of green chutney. It was fluffy, light and tasty, which is perhaps why Kannadigas opt for this dosa all the time.

When I had breakfast with Kannadiga friends recently at MTR (Mahalakshmi Tiffin Room), they all chose the khali dosa over the masala dosa. Why, I asked, because to me, the khali dosa is a poor cousin of the ghee-laden rich masala dosa. The answer is as nuanced as the Kannadiga people themselves. They like the fluffiness of the khali dosa. They believe it is healthy because it requires less oil. It is easier on the stomach. Plus, if your routine involves a morning walk in Lalbagh followed by dosa at a darshini (when people think of Bangalore food, they don't think of five-star hotels but what we call 'darshinis'), you had better choose the khali dosa. Sure, you are eating carbs but at least one with less oil.

So it was that our group polished off the khali dosas and began walking to our next stop: Davanagere benne (butter) dosa. Davanagere is located pretty much in the centre of Karnataka, which explains why it is called the 'heart of Karnataka'. The state's culinary diversity is represented in this town. Like all creation stories, the 'benne dosa' or butter dosa too begins with an old woman who invented this type of soft fluffy dosa, smaller than the average dosa, sprinkled with chutney powder on the inside, folded over and served with a generous dollop of butter and aloo palya on the side. This came to be called the benne dosa and today you see outlets selling Davanagere benne dosa all over Bangalore. They are more common in South Bangalore.

The thing with a benne dosa is that it inspires extreme opinions. One dosa-loving friend hates benne dosas because she says that they always are too crisp. Even though I don't hate butter dosas, I have to agree with her on the crispiness. The outlet we went to scored points before I even had a bite for one reason: the sign was entirely in Kannada. I took a photo of it and then through some sleuthing using its location, I discovered that its name is Sri Guru Kottureshwara Davanagere Benne Dosa. We had the dosa of course, all ten of us. Shared it 'by two' as is common in Bangalore. I was delighted to see that they also sold a few Kannadiga specialties, about which I have written about: girmit, mandakki avalakki, nargis avalakki, mensinakai bajji, and of course the benne dosa. I tried the mandakki and it was a bit soggy. The benne dosa though was brilliant—not too crispy, not too spicy. I always find the potato palya (what we call our sabzis) a bit bland compared to ones in Tamilnadu. But my group loved it.

Our third stop was Namma SLN, a tiny storefront in Gandhi Bazaar. It was here that I had, for the first time, a sabakki (dill) idli and dosa. Both were heavenly and I recommend them highly. When I searched for 'sabakki' on the internet to find the recipe, I found that what Kannadigas call sabakki is actually sabudana or tapioca pearls. These are soaked and ground into a dosa batter. To this, chopped dill is added. Dill is called sabsige soppu in Kannada. It is used in many recipes including rice roti or akki roti, and a variety of palyas or curries, and also a rasam called sabsige soppu saaru. Saaru means a watery soup and it is made with a variety of greens and vegetables. Our group enjoyed the sabakki masala dosa served extremely sustainably on a banana leaf backed by another stronger leaf. I loved the sabakki idli. It was redolent of dill and soft as a mother's touch.

Basavanagudi is a place but it is also a feeling. It is a timeless vision of what old Bangalore used to be like with street vendors selling flowers, fruits and vegetables; neighbourhood aunties and uncles walking with their bags to bargain with vendors before heading to the temple in the mornings; and young children who were watched by the entire neighbourhood as they played on the streets. This was the Bangalore I visited as a child when I came to my uncle's house in Rajaji Nagar, and it still exists in parts of Bangalore including Basavanagudi.

Kaali dal and corner cafes: Bangalore's take on Delhi delights

Bangalore is sweltering this week, one in which we are reading about eclipses and looking for the crescent-shaped moon. Eid al-Fitr marks the end of the holy month of Ramadan. As a vegetarian, it makes me jealous to hear friends rave about the haleem, and the nihari that they enjoyed during *iftar* this year. I gorged on *shahi tukda*, which to my mind is the queen of desserts, amongst the many that are served in the night markets around Mosque Road.

This week also marks the beginning of a new year or Yug-adi. With it comes the *pachadi*, a cooling mixture with six different tastes, made with tamarind, mango, jaggery, neem flowers, salt and pepper. Six tastes to prepare you for the six flavours—from bitter to sweet—that life will hand out so that you can swallow them all with sanguinity.

Mostly, what I have been swallowing is rich Indian food. Bangalore is in the throes of so many new restaurant openings. But this isn't a survey of Burma Burma, Koko, Muro, Moglu, Lyfe, Oota, Oura, Navu and so many other standalone restaurants. This is about the revival of North Indian cuisine in Bangalore.

For a long time, ITC Windsor's Royal Afghan was the uncrowned champion of North Indian *khana.* They had it down pat—everything from the consistency of taste to the quality of the plating. Everything was uniform and pleasingly predictable, to the point where a friend asked, 'Is ITC the McDonald's of Indian food? And he meant it as a compliment. But now there are other five-stars who are stepping into the ring.

Last week, I went to Zarf, a new North Indian restaurant in faraway Whitefield. Helmed by Chef J.P. Singh who used to be at the Leela Bharatiya City, Zarf's kali-dal was delicious. More than one foodie pronounced it the best in the city, over ITC's version—which is saying a lot.

My brother took us for my Mom's birthday lunch to Loya, the newish restaurant at the Taj West End. The food was delicious, and the drinks, even more so. We all drank a couple of cocktails made with mint, citrus and mango. All of us were in her happy place. The Ritz-Carlton has Riwaz which I used to frequent, but now go to its Lantern Chinese restaurant. The Leela's Jamawar was a favourite of the corporate crowd—still is, in fact. And Falak in faraway Leela Bharatiya City aspired to make the best tandoori chicken in the country. Even the Four Seasons, known for its pan-Asian restaurant, is hosting Awadhi nights. Central Bangalore hotels like the Conrad and the Oberoi do their best, but no one so far has been able to dethrone ITC. Which begs the question: what does a fine-dining North Indian restaurant have to do to capture the imagination of the dining public? How can you create a signature when all the signature dishes have been 'chaapa-ed' or stamped by one hotel chain?

To arrive at the answer, I take a detour. Last week, my cousin called from the US in great excitement. The Queens temple canteen had made it to the *New York Times*' annual list of top 100 restaurants in New York, he said. It was No. 80 and Semma, run by South Indian chef Vijay Kumar, was No. 5. The only other two Indian restaurants on the list were Dhamaka and Hyderabadi Zaiqa. To get on the list, these restaurants need to take a different route than what they would do in India. They need to do modern, fusion, recalibrated Indian to suit an adventurous, largely Western palate. In India, most fusion restaurants that take risks die.

For Indian restaurants—and for purposes of the subject in this chapter, let us limit it to North Indian restaurants because there are very few South Indian fine-dining restaurants except Dakshin, which even I as a South Indian find boring. I cannot think of a South Indian five-star restaurant that I would opt for on a Sunday. But there are many North Indian places that we go to, beginning with Tandoor, the old favourite on M.G. Road.

The problem is that all these restaurants suffer from what economists call 'confirmation bias'. They have seen that what succeeds in the Indian market is heavy, rich, Mughlai food with lots of butter, chicken, kebabs, marination, paneer, gravy and general gooey-ness. So nobody thinks to do subtle anymore. Nobody thinks of presenting in a new way. Zarf does a tableside tempering of the classic yellow dal—somewhat like how Mexican restaurants do tableside guacamole. It's a nice touch but

I imagine that it can get old fast, particularly if you are in a party of friends and the server sort of demands that you stop speaking to witness the drama of dal.

To me, the next bastion of North Indian food is to look to the light flavours of U.P. vegetarian food—its variety of dals that go beyond the usual yellow and kaali dal; its subtle, restrained use of spices; and its adventurous use of vegetables that go beyond the navratan kurma-type ones. What about the gourds that are native to India? What about jackfruit beyond using it as mock-meat? What about morels and other mushrooms without dunking them in too much sauce? If rich North Indian was the past, why not make subtle and restrained North Indian the future?

Is Bangalore India's artisanal pizza capital?

The best pizza I have eaten in Bangalore is at my friend Jay Bhow's house. So when Jay, a VPN -certified pizzaiolo, wondered if Bangalore was the artisanal pizza capital of India, we decided to go on a pizza crawl to find out. Over two days we dined at seven pizza restaurants. Our method was to try the Margherita at every outlet we visited—always a benchmark. We also ordered their signature pizza—a highlight of the establishment. Turned out that all the places we visited suggested vegetarian pizzas as one of their signature offerings. So even though there were non-vegetarians in our group of four, we ended up eating all vegetarian pizzas, often with wine. Below are some of our tasting notes.

Pizza 4Ps has been making waves in Bangalore for a while and with good reason. Their burrata salad pizza was brilliant—tart, creamy and crunchy. The crust, which sets a benchmark of 'pass or fail' in artisanal pizza, was chewy with perfect bubbly air pockets in the rim. The bottom of the crust had charred, black 'leopard spots', giving the woody flavour. I found the Margherita's crust to be slightly soggy but the toppings were layered with a restrained hand. Often Indian pizzas are over-laden with cheese because the clientele demands it. Not here. Good selection of local wine, though their glasses could be better.

23rd Street Pizza gets a lot of things right. It serves New York-style pizza (in which olive oil is mixed into the dough) with a medium, not thin crust. It is served on a pizza stand on an aluminium (not wood) platter, just like in New York. It even gets the checked paper below the pizza right. The Pick me Up pizza, their signature, was spicy and piquant. Their Margherita too was well-balanced. What pleased us was their wine list. Tightly curated and served in beautiful glasses, we enjoyed the white and red wines by the glass.

La Gioia is a new kid in town and needs to be marketed better. The staff and the chef are clearly passionate about pizza. When they learned that Jay was a pizzaiolo, they began comparing Italian products, tomatoes and sauces. They have artefacts from Italy and interesting utensils, but the ambience inside could be livelier. The pizzas were made with mozzarella fior di latte, made from cow's milk rather than buffalo. They do homemade pastas too—so worth a visit.

Trippy Goat, with its café vibe, is not a pizza restaurant or even an Italian one, but it has a gas-fired pizza oven. It is here, when talking to the owner, that we learned about the compromises that pizza restaurants had to make for the Indian palate—adding extra cheese on the topping, for one. Try the terrific mushroom pizza with truffle oil drizzled on top. They have a lot of interesting wines by the glass that go with the pizza in Schott Zwiesel glasses.

Brik Oven was the original Bangalore pizzeria. It is arguably the most authentic, since it is completely wood-fired, as opposed to most of the others here that are gas-fired. This gives the pizzas a nice smoky, charred flavour. The tiny space on Church Street makes up for in food what it lacks in ambience. Try their mushroom and arugula one. On the pizza crawl, we had the perfectly good Margherita and a terrific Diavola with sliced baby eggplant, bird's eye chilli, sundried tomatoes and feta. They also have a terrific vegan list of pizzas and milkshakes.

Spettacolore is a vegetarian Italian restaurant that does not serve alcohol. Choose the al fresco seating overlooking some trees. Order yourself a Diet Coke—goes great with pizza anyway. But this is a place that takes ingredients seriously, using Italian 00 flour—the standard—and allowing the pizza dough to ferment for 40–50 hours. They make their mozzarella and other cheeses in-house. Besides Neapolitan, they also do a Canotto-style pizza where the crust has a bigger rim, giving it a canoe-like effect with the toppings in the centre.

Whenever I go to Lyfe in Whitefield, I try their Jay's Special Bianco pizza, named after—who else—Jay Bhow. With red onion, parmesan, bocconcini, rosemary and almond flakes, it is a terrific change from the red sauce-based pizzas available everywhere. This time, because we knew the chef-owner, Abhijit Saha, I tried making a pizza under Jay's watchful eye. Making pizza is both easy and hard. The dough is forgiving but requires a firm touch, a muscle memory. You need to pat the dough—like bajra roti—and spread it evenly. I made a pesto topping and layered some colourful bell peppers—red, yellow and green—on it. Had a hard time getting the slippery pizza on the long handle to shove it into the oven. All of which made me grasp and respect the process of making pizza a whole lot more.

⁂

In Bangalore, food is just the start: Fine dining, art, music, and AI

When you go to a restaurant, what do you go for? If it is just food, I would argue that you can get better food at your home or a relative's home. Most of us go for the experience, the theatre, the presentation, the service, the feeling of being cosseted. This is what we pay for. The question is, how much premium are you willing to pay for this?

For restaurants in luxury hotels, this becomes a key question. 'The problem is that there are too many standalone restaurants competing for customers,' said one luxury hotel's general manager ruefully.

It's true. The Bangalore restaurant scene is surging with new openings, many of them brewpubs. Standalone restaurants are packed, even on weekdays. This is normal in Delhi and Mumbai, but Bangalore was considered to be a sleepy city. Not anymore. These days, Bangalore is changing from an IT-driven city to one that is embracing the good life. Given the competition, hoteliers and restauranteurs have to figure out how to get footfalls.

The Ritz Carlton Bengaluru decided to use animation and AI to create an immersive experience. They have partnered with a global outfit called Dinner Tales to create a story called 'Banquet of Hoshena'. Frankly, when I attended this banquet, it had too much 'jing-bang', as we call it, for me to pay attention to the storyline—about kings and queens. There were levitating dishes, candles that lit when you pointed at them, a ceramic statue of a lady whose eyes moved, projected flowers on the table cloth, speaking plates. Kids would love all this. Depending on your point of view, this takes fine-dining to the next level or distracts from the food. The contemporary Indian food created by chefs Anupam Gulati and Imran worked hard to stand up to the overstimulation, and largely succeeded. Conversation too is interrupted by the story, so if you want an intimate uninterrupted meal, this is not for you. This experience would be perfect for corporates though, because you can wow your colleagues or clients without having to engage in too much chit-chat.

Another approach is live acts. On Mother's Day, the Four Seasons introduced a monthly Sunday brunch with a mix of music, food, art and wellness. Music is already part of Sunday brunches, although I wish they would keep the volume of the live music low. How then to add more layers to the Sunday brunch? Art and pampering seem to be the approach adopted by the Four Seasons. They partnered with Art 'n Soul, whose tagline on Instagram says 'empowering female creatives globally'. The way this is done is through hotels, many in Scandinavia, and also through global brands like Soho House, Milan Design

Week, and now the Four Seasons. Two musicians, Akshita Mengi and Gowri Bhat, sang a mix of Carnatic, R&B, folk and pop. I personally am waiting for Bangalore hotels to invite folk musicians who will mix some Kannada with their songs. Artist Aanchal Gupta painted live alongside the music. In a corner, Shankara, a cosmetics brand, offered foot and hand massages with a soft-sell of their ayurvedic products. You could walk around between courses, get a massage, listen to music and watch the painter.

The thing though is that this state's cuisine is more than the idli and dosa. This point was made to me at a recent food festival that MTR Foods organized. The advertisement said that there would be over 100 dishes, all vegetarian. I must have eaten every single item. I could do this because the portions were small with throwaway eco-friendly leaf-plates. I drank wood-apple juice and piquant kokum rasam, had jowar roti with a variety of brinjal preparations, and spongy steamed *sanna*s wrapped in jackfruit leaves, and tasted a mind-boggling array of chutneys. Heard of bilimbi chutney? It is a sour citrusy fruit about half the size of a melon. Made into chutney, it goes well with the millets that are the mainstay of Uttara Karnataka. The Kodagu (Coorg) section had a vegetarian option. It is called 'moodaray kanee', a soup made with horse gram. I dislike horse gram in general, but this soup/kanji, I could drink every day. Yes, I know, it is a poor cousin to the famous Kodagu Pandi (pork) curry that we vegetarians cannot eat. And so it went at every counter—representing the regions of Karnataka. Something new, others familiar, always fresh and healthy.

The food of this state is super-healthy. Most people don't know that, but it really is the foodie takeaway of this column.

❧

Forks for Delhi, fingers for Bangalore: The geography of eating

Is South Indian food more messy than North Indian food, or is it more sensual? Is it because we eat on a banana leaf which is to food what the napkin/ plate/tablecloth combo is for other foods? Is it because North India brings out its katori army, arranged like chess pieces, with one bowl for each dish? Is it because our gravies—think sambar, olan and stew—are more runny than their rajma or rogan josh? How does India eat and why does it eat this way? Is it because restaurants have changed how we eat or is it intrinsic to the food?

Chef Sara Jacob links it to the North Indian 'katori system' versus the South Indian eating on a banana leaf. Sara is in Bangalore to do a pop-up called Nair on Fire at Lush restaurant in Renaissance Bengaluru Race Course Hotel. She specializes in Kerala cuisine that she markets through Instagram with celebrity endorsements and restaurant pop-ups across the country. Sara tells me how the pop-ups she does in Delhi are different from the ones she does in Bangalore. In Delhi, she says, she arranges her dishes in neat layers, allowing for people to use a fork and spoon. In Bangalore, she doesn't have to do any of this, serving her eriseri, puliseri, olan and stews in mud pots. The dozen-odd people at my table all mix the dishes by hand without any self-consciousness and are clearly enjoying themselves, which is why I asked the original question: is South Indian food more messy than North Indian food?

'Not messy. More sensual,' says Chef Regi Mathew, who runs Kappa Chakka Kandhari in Bangalore and Chennai. He describes all the ways in which we use our fingers, which are intuitive and natural to me. In South India, we are not shy about eating. We use our entire hand to work with the food. We have the concept of 'pesanju', which is mixing and mashing with our fingers. It is supremely sensual, I agree, but it also looks messy. There are many advantages to this method of eating. Using your hands tells you the temperature of the food—if it is too hot to put in your mouth. You can mix a banana with the Kerala puttu in this same manner, allowing the mashed banana to leak through your fingers, giving you the pleasant sensation of feeling the cold banana with the hot puttu. My North Indian friends cannot stand to even see this leaking banana between my fingers, let alone emulate it.

North Indians also have an aversion to using the palms of their hands, perhaps because theirs is more of a roti culture rather than a rice culture. Sure, they use their hands to eat but tend to stick to delicately touching food with the tips of their fingers rather than the, shall I say, more robust way in which South Indians eat. I have known Chennai weddings where we all licked our entire palm when it was coated with curd rice or payasam. To eat a runny rasam-rice with your hand involves a deft centrifugal movement in which you somehow contain the rapidly running rasam-rice into the palms of your hand and then quickly down it in one lick, like a serpent swallowing a vole. This vainglorious (some would call it inglorious) method of eating comes naturally to us in South India, perhaps because we weren't subject to waves of invasion. We are not self-conscious about our ways.

Some part of it is also familiarity, as food consultant Aslam Gafoor says. People in Old Delhi are very comfortable eating parathas with their hands in a manner that can also be called messy. But take them to a restaurant and they will use the spoon. So, are restaurants the real culprits? Are they the ones who have changed how India eats? I think there is some truth to that. The five-star restaurants of India take their cue from their Western counterparts and—with a few exceptions—expect us to eat Indian dishes with a fork and spoon. This is true of the five-star Indian restaurant-chains like Bukhara, Jamavar, Loya and others.

Familiarity with the cuisine is the other factor. The same North Indians who eat chole-bhature with their hands will eat upma (a South Indian dish) with a spoon. South Indians, on the other hand, have an aversion to the spoon.

Sure, I haven't mentioned the other parts of India, but I think the divisions are clear. Katori or banana leaf, rice or roti, fingers or palms, runny gravy or thick, invasions or not. These determine your eating habits.

∞

The contradictory challenges of star-chefs who visit Bangalore

To be a good chef, you have to have knowledge, opinion and confidence. Few professions are as unforgiving as a chef's chosen job. You get feedback instantly. If the dish isn't good, it gets sent back to the kitchen. Reviews appear on platforms and word-of-mouth criticism spreads like wildfire. No wonder most chefs develop an armour to shield and protect them. Recently, a number of star-chefs have been visiting Bangalore. Here then is my take on the ones that I have dined at.

Gaggan Anand was in Bangalore recently for a pop-up, titled 'The Royal Homecoming', at the JW Marriott Prestige Golfshire's Indian outlet, Aaleeshan. Anand is a master at compressing flavours and serving chameleon-like dishes. The idli-sambar looked like a cupcake and burst with flavours of chutney, milagai-podi and fermented idli. The bhelpuri looked like a soan-papdi. The 'yogurt explosion' wobbled like jelly but was white like yogurt. This type of sleight-of-hand surprises is what Anand is known for and he did not disappoint. He is also passionate about

Indian food and has a point of view about how it should be served and presented. He has chefs he likes—Floyd Cardoz, and chefs he dislikes. He articulates his view with passion and precision. He is a gifted chef who ought to spend more time in India.

Prateek Sadhu is a chef who has received a lot of press and has taken a laudable risk by opening Naar, a 14-seater restaurant in Kasauli. He was at The Leela Palace Bengaluru recently, where he began his career. The seven-course meal was paired with Ardmore cocktails. The thing with tasting menus is the pacing of the food and service. Sadhu and the service team at the Leela managed to keep the pacing brisk, bringing out course after course in choreographed unison. Highlights included the dishes redolent of mustard sourced from the hills, the gucchi/morel mushrooms and many other local ingredients that the team had brought along from Kasauli. This is the pleasure of a pop-up: access to dishes and ingredients that are not normally available. There wasn't any one standout dish, at least not one that I recall in the way that I can Gaggan Anand's surprising flavours and presentation.

The Oberoi brought down the chef and bartender from its standalone Mumbai restaurant, Amadeo, for a few days, perhaps testing the waters to see if a Bangalore audience would be receptive to the Indian, Italian and Chinese cuisines that populate Amadeo's menu. The ever-smiling chef Kayzad Sadri exuded humility. Women bartenders have been winning awards—is it because their palate is finer—and so it was with Swarangi, the bartender that day, who mixed creative cocktails. The truffle tagliatelle was the standout dish for me. Salad pizza is hard to eat without looking silly. The duck seekh kebab, said my friend, was terrific. My vegetarian gucchi makhana was wonderful too, but the best gucchi dish I have eaten recently was at Loya at the Taj West End—they mostly serve the morel generously. Desserts at the Oberoi tasting were terrific. I don't like ice-cream, and dislike chocolate ice-cream (I know, don't ask), but the Amadeo ice-cream was perfect—not too creamy or too sweet.

Kerwin Savio Nigli, the head of the department of hotel management at Christ University, invited a group of us for a 47-course vegetarian Onam Sadhya put together by his students. Laid out on a humble banana leaf, the feast displayed ambition and creativity. The payasam served as dessert was made with garlic, the halwa made of tomato. None of us could guess the ingredients. There were a number of traditional dishes, prepared well. Most were good. I couldn't bite into the Colocasia patrode because it was too fibrous. The moringa rice, millet bisi bele bhaath, and bite-size quantities of the many fresh sabzis and palyas were excellent. There were hundreds of students who lined up to serve us, so pacing wasn't an issue at all. They had dances and music as entertainment. I would have loved to know more about the students and their ambitions—what the class wanted to do and what brought them to their chosen profession. The Onam kolam/rangoli made with grains offered a creative twist.

Hospitality, whether in the kitchen or in the dining hall, involves a contradiction. On the one hand, you have to please the palates of your customers, which requires a talent for service and the desire to please. On the other, it also requires you to guide the diners towards places and dishes where they may not want to go, which requires an instinct for leadership and some amount of moxie. How the chefs and service team balance guiding and serving can make or break the dining experience. Not all get it right.

The best cheese and bread in Bangalore

There is a day in mid-April that happens to be World Malbec Day, an entirely manufactured celebration, brazenly marketed as a 'world' event, when in fact it was created by Argentina to promote their Malbec grape. Heck, it worked. Today Malbec wine is synonymous with Argentina.

What this highlights is how poorly we market India. Shouldn't we have World Turmeric Day, now that people in California are downing turmeric shots and golden lattes? Why aren't we out claiming global days and world events for our mudras, mantras and all the healing arts that India invented? The West has co-opted yoga to the point where the only thing Indian in a yoga class outside our country is the obligatory Namaste said in a jarring unrecognizable accent at the end of the class.

To drown these sorrows, I decided to open an Argentinian Malbec and ponder the injustices of cultural appropriation. Poet Omar Khayyam had his priorities right. A long time ago, he said, rather philosophically (but oh, how grounded in the good things of life) in his Rubaiyat, 'a jug of wine, a loaf of bread and thou…' To this sentence, I would also add cheese.

Used to be a time when the only cheese that Indians ate—and that too, doled out suspiciously by Moms, at least in South India—was Amul. Today, a variety of solid, serviceable cheeses are available in India. I like buying local cheeses but until recently have not had a good experience with them. Frankly, they taste alike, and are only labelled differently and rather optimistically as cheddar, brie, camembert and so on. My local Thoms Supermarket stocks Kodai cheeses. The A2 milk I buy from Akshayakalpa also makes cheeses that I order via their app. They all have that stringy heaviness that is typical of cheeses, but are good only to make chilli cheese toast rather than put on a cheese board.

The problem with Indian cheeses is that they aren't aged long enough or well enough. So they don't have the sharp differentiated taste that is typical of excellent European cheeses. India's hot temperature and power cuts mean that the delicate bacterial cultures that add flavour to cheeses are not able to do their work gradually and gracefully. The result is that hard cheeses mostly taste like paneer ++ and soft cheeses taste like nothing. Cheddar isn't sharp and blue cheese isn't funky-tasting enough.

That assessment has changed with this latest lot of Indian cheeses I sampled. Eleftheria is Mumbai-based and arguably has the widest selection of artisanal cheeses in the country. Their award-winning brunost looks like brown caramel and tastes like a weird but strangely winning combination of cheese and fudge. I loved their soft cheeses. Melchior doesn't do much marketing beyond 'French guy in Bengaluru making cheese', but that is an understatement. Consider his Dutch-style Gouda, cutely called Kempe Gouda, in honour of the city it is made in.

In Koramangala, cheese-loving friends frequent Nari & Kage (Kannada words meaning Fox & Crow), a tiny fromagerie selling cheeses in wooden boxes. Cheese boards from Onboard Blr and Graze Box by Kavana Kariappa make entertaining easy with their pre-made and pretty-looking charcuterie. There are vegan cheeses often sold in marketplaces and pop-ups curated by Namu Kini. I used to buy Angelo's Cheeses and am searching for the next big thing.

To eat cheese, you need bread. Bangalore is blessed in this area because we have many gifted bakers. For a long time, I have bought bread from Honore Bakery run by Ponnanna, a weekly ritual when my kids were young. Now I have expanded my repertoire somewhat. I go to Lavonne Bakery in Domlur to buy their tiramisu and almond croissants. At wine writer, Ruma Singh's home, I ate a dense gluten-free bread from Loafer & Co, and so I began buying the same seeded loaf to eat with my cheeses. Backer & Charlie in Sindhi Colony serves German-style pretzels, dark rye bread and sandwiches. Krumbkraft makes great sourdough, although why this specific bread is so popular in India awaits analysis. Sourhouse founder Selvan Thandapani loves fermenting in all its forms. He sells bread but also kombucha and is generous with tips. Chez Mariannick has been a fixture in Whitefield: all my home baker friends in that area swear by her.

So, which is the best bread in Bangalore? Well, that

depends. My mom still buys her soft half loaf from a no-name local bakery that only does bread. Albert Bakery in Frazer Town is famous for its pastry-like khoya naans. As for Iyengar bakeries, Bangalore probably has the best Iyengar bakeries in the country but that requires a separate column.

Cocktails and Kalpavriksh: Balancing inventiveness and restraint

The problem with creating cocktails in India is that we have *too* many ingredients available to us. I mean, think about it. For an imaginative mixologist, this throws up a dizzying array of choices and not all of them good. The best cocktails are like a great piece of sculpture: they are all about structure and spirit. They play within boundaries, within a limited palette, and allow the spirit to soar with just a shade of storytelling. This is difficult in India because we have too many spices, too many aromatics, and too many fruits and flowers, all of which, in theory, would enhance a cocktail. They might but only in the right hands. Classic cocktails have three, maybe four, ingredients. They don't infuse and confuse. They don't extract and subtract. They don't show off and put you off. But here then is the paradox. Cocktails are also pretty and fun. They are not serious drinks to be imbibed in silence. They are social drinks that you clink on a night out with friends.

How then to stay true to the spirit of, well, spirits and yet spritz it up appropriately?

The answer is restraint. A great cocktail is like a flamenco dance. It looks fantastic and fun but it is in actuality about appropriateness: about striking a pose where you half-face the audience; about giving them just enough. If you ask the amateur about flamenco, they will think of drama. But great flamenco dancers know that the signature of this flamboyant dance form is actually restraint. The well-placed gesture at the end of all that tapping. Which, when you think about it, should also define a great cocktail. Lots of drama, lots of tapping, tossing, stirring and shaking. Lots of flamboyance. But in the end, just the perfect balance that operates within understood boundaries.

For a long time, my pet peeve was that cocktails in India were largely copycats: the names, the ingredients, the flavours, everything. In this, I wasn't alone. If you get together with any bartender or mixologist, the talk eventually ends up at reinventing cocktails so that 'Indian cocktails' take over the world—just like Indian food, textiles, music, movies, you name it. We want to be the best. The problem is that reinvention is such a large canvas. There are so many ways to do this; so many permutations and combinations—again, not all of them good.

Names, for example, are a good place to start. You can mess with them to a certain extent. Raahi Neo Kitchen and Bar, for instance, deserves points for using the navarasas (nine emotions) of Indian dance as a jump-off point, but really, I had no idea what it meant till I read the subhead. The Sakkath martini in SOKA does it better because it doffs a hat to that ubiquitous Kannada slang-word while telling you what you are drinking. Jammin Goat probably has the worst names for its good cocktails: Future Water, Perspective, Sudden Orgasm, all sound like inside jokes but don't answer the basic question in any cocktail: what's the spirit?

Beyond names, it comes to ingredients, which is where things get crazy. Using Indian ingredients in cocktails is tempting. All the top bars do it. Copitas uses betel leaves in its 'Leaf' cocktail—again, you have no idea what the base spirit is unless you read the sub-heading. The 'Flower' rum has Kerala tamarind or kudam-puli. I like its 'Fruit' cocktail the best because it uses restraint in the play of ingredients with just black-lemon spiking the gin. Plus, the view from the bar is sweeping and lovely at sunset.

In terms of sheer beauty, the ZLB23 at the Leela Palace Bengaluru perhaps holds the candle. The space is reminiscent of the sets in that classic Wong Kar-Wai movie, *In the Mood for Love.* ZLB23 bills itself as a Kyoto Speakeasy and does 'technical' cocktails with lots of extractions. Like everywhere in India, here too, gin and tequila are the spirits of the moment. There were many interesting cocktails—I wished someone in Bangalore would start the idea of a cocktail flight with small portions of multiple drinks. It makes a lot of sense if you go in with a group. You can try out several cocktails before choosing what you like. Beer and wine have flights, why not cocktails? The staff at ZLB23 is 80 per cent female, which is something that its general manager, Madhav Sehgal, has been spearheading through his many efforts including 'Shefs at The Leela'. If Sehgal manages to increase female participation in his workforce, then hats off to him.

Two of the bartenders of the moment happen to be women. When I visited ZLB23, Priyanka Mondal had just won the Prowein 'Bartender of the Year' award and was away in London and later, Bangkok. Pune-based bartender Aashi Bhatnagar (her Instagram handle spells it as Aashie) is the winner of the 2023 Diageo World Class, which Vikram Achanta, co-founder of Tulleeho and 30 Best Bars India, calls the 'Oscars' of bartending. Do women have a more sensitive palate than men? Some studies say so and if this is the case, will these two women who are at the top of their game manage the balancing act between innovation and tradition?

The best advice that I follow when I make cocktails is what German architect Ludwig Mies Van Der Rohe said about buildings and beauty: less is more.

Is beer the butter chicken of Bangalore?

When in Bangalore, do yourself a favour. Go into one of the 85 craft breweries in the city—or rather, try to go, because depending on the day, you won't be able to get in. Weekends 'tho', as we say in Hindi, forget it. And these aren't small places. In order to get a microbrewery licence, you need 10,000 square feet at minimum. Beginning Thursday night, craft breweries are packed. Hence my question: is beer the butter chicken of Bangalore? All parts of this question are operative.

You see, I am a serious wine drinker (not a pretentious one though) and a casual beer drinker. In the wine world, we keep talking about how India is ground-zero for the wine business, and how more and more young Indians are drinking wine. But that's because we haven't seen the growth spurt in the craft beer industry. No other alcoholic beverage has been able to forge such a huge fan base amongst Indians—and Bangaloreans. So, to all my wine-drinking friends, I say, we winos are living in la-la land.

Beer—not wine—is taking over the Indian subcontinent. Part of the reason is because wine is viewed as elitist while beer is accessible, without fuss. Like butter chicken, it is a crowd pleaser that doesn't take itself too seriously. And now we come to the title of this essay.

Please read the question again. I am not talking about foods that *pair* well with beer. Of that, there are many including pakoras, peanuts, vadas, fried food in general, biriyani, Andhra meals, spicy food in general—heck, all Indian food except maybe our sweets. Is food pairing the secret of beer's success? Maybe.

Years ago, I got really mad when a Western wine writer wrote that the best wine pairing with Indian food was, well, 'beer'. I thought he was dissing India's wine palate, our country's sophistication with respect to wine, and that he displayed typical Western chauvinism when it came to new cultures savouring wine. Now that I have started drinking craft beers in Bangalore, I have to admit that he may be right and take that chip off my shoulder. Indian food pairs really well with a chilled beer.

That said, what Indian dish do you associate most with beer? If beer were an Indian dish, which one would it be? I can only think of three contenders and I have never tasted two of them: butter chicken, tandoori chicken, and masala dosa.

Now I have written a lot about masala dosa, but this dish is too parochial and dare I say, Brahminical, to align with beer. Bangalore, much like beer, is cosmopolitan, forgiving and welcoming. Masala dosa is too entrenched and regional. That leaves the two chicken dishes, which I, as a lifelong vegetarian, have never tasted. But if I were to eat non-veg, I would probably begin with these two dishes. They look appetizing. A friend told me eat them just before I die because then my regret for not eating chicken earlier would last for a shorter period of time. Twisted logic—but then this friend is a serious carnivore.

Beer and butter chicken have a lot in common. Take the dish. Originally from Punjab, butter chicken has taken over the world, much like beer. Both adapt well to regional variations. Butter chicken is touted as the national dish of the UK. I would reckon that the English version is nothing like the fiery Telangana version. Much like beer, butter chicken lends itself to fine-dining and dhabas. Both beer and butter chicken are ancient inventions, and perhaps they were created around the same time.

Today Belgium, Germany, the Czech Republic and England are the four countries that come to mind when you think of beer. Except that these guys eat food that is nothing like our spicy Indian food. German sausages, Czech dumplings, English shepherd's pie and Belgian steak frites are the opposite of our spicy food. Yet somehow, our food pairs just as well with beer as do the weak-kneed non-spicy food of these Northern European countries. We have to grant them one thing though. Northern European countries were the pioneers in elevating beer into the dry-hopped, barrel-aged, limited-release, small-batch artisanal versions that are taking over India.

This then is the genius of beer, relative to my other drink: wine. Even though beer is arguably more complex than wine; even though it definitely takes more steps to make beer than wine, beer wears its laurels lightly.

It is forgiving when it comes to food pairings. Throw a kheema kebab at a white wine and the wine will wilt. Throw a kheema kebab at a German Kolsch and it will dance. In fact, I cannot think of a single variety of beer, be it a Belgian ale, German lager, Czech Pilsner, or Irish Stout, that *won't* go with Indian food. Beer therefore is like butter chicken: complex yet accessible.

Where do I go to drink my beer in Bangalore? Well, that requires a separate article.

Bar hopping in Bangalore: An authoritative guide

Best wine bars and microbreweries for a pint of beer in India's startup capital

Any article that claims to be an authoritative guide should be viewed with a jaundiced eye, preferably after a couple of beers. So too with this one, which began with me looking for 'beer jokes'. The only halfway decent one was this: Why did the beer go to therapy? Because it had problems with its head.

Depending on who you ask, beer was brewed 12,000 years ago in various regions of the world, just about when humans were domesticating chickens and figuring out agriculture. They had grains, and naturally, leftover grain attracted yeast from the air and fermented. From there, it was just a short hop to the addition of hops. Both China and Sumeria can lay claim to crafting beer but it was the Bavarians (northern Germans) and Bohemians (Czech folks) who perfected the modern version. India has no specific beer tradition—any ancient references begin and end with Soma. Country liquor and spirits are a different matter, and here we find them in the Northeast, Goa, and many other parts of India. But rice beer isn't exactly beer, at least not as we understand it in its modern avatar.

Within India, Bangalore can lay claim to a beer connection primarily because Kingfisher—still beloved or berated depending on who you ask—was brewed here. Today, Bangalore has more breweries than any other city. But thanks to its horrendous traffic, most people drink close to home, forcing breweries to open branches in different areas. Here then is an incomplete guide to what you can drink where.

Regarding wine, lots of people ask about wine bars in Bangalore. The short answer is there aren't many. There are restaurants with wine lists but very few wine bars of note. This is a pity because just outside Bangalore are well known wineries such as Grover's and Big Banyan.

To that end, I only have a couple of wine bar recommendations, relative to the brewery ones. To create the brewery list, I went on pub-crawls, consulted numerous winemakers and master-brewers for their opinions, but in the end I relied on a few friends who are ardent drinkers. They have no commercial stake in the game and are therefore neutral drinkers. They include Vishal Joshi, who works at an e-commerce firm and says that he has drunk beer in every outlet in the city. He regularly goes on beer-crawls in different neighbourhoods. The second is Devesh Agarwal, who founded The Wine Connoisseurs, a wine-drinking club in the city, and is now rediscovering beer. The third is V. Sanjay Kumar, an author and wine/

beer drinker. Using their inputs along with those from brewery owners, here then is a list. I will start with the few wine bar recommendations before moving to the beer.

1. Wine in Progress: This is a new wine bar at The Courtyard and has potential. It aims to be wine-forward even though its wine list is only two pages. At least it has a CWO—Chief Wine Officer.
2. Trippy Goat: This central Bangalore restaurant has a well-chosen wine list and a cellar next door where you can buy bottles of wine.
3. Fox in the Field: One of the owners, Abhay Kewadkar has been involved with wine for decades. If you catch him in-house, have a beer and talk to him about wine.
4. Toscano: This was one of the earliest wine-friendly restaurants. It continues to have a good wine list and locations throughout the city.
5. Lyfe: Chef Abhijit Saha is respected amongst Bangalore food lovers. His new restaurant with its tight wine list makes the trek to Whitefield worthwhile.
6. Longboat Brewing Co: Consistent pilsners and IPAs. Brewmaster Karthik Singh tells us that the best time to drink a craft IPA is just a couple of days after it is brewed. Owner Girish Prahlada loves Karnataka snacks and ensures that Bangalore's chaklis, peanuts and churmuris are served as appetizers along with ghee roast chicken and paneer.
7. Geist Brewing Co: Founded by Narayan Manepally, with three outlets within the city, Geist sells its craft beers in oxygen-free crowlers. Enthusiasts brave traffic

to enjoy its Kama Citra IPA, Weiss Guy and Uncle Dunkle. Brew master Vidya Kubher has mentored many. The brand brought together six women brewers in Geist's wonderful 'Ladies who Lager' initiative.

8. Biergarten in Koramangala and Whitefield: Brew master Lalit Vijay prefers 'clean' flavours in beer but is unafraid of trial and error. His experiments include a lovely Alt, Smoked Pineapple Sour, Ragi Ale, and a Super Dry which enthusiasts call LSD (Lalit's Super Dry). I loved Vijay's pilsners with its 'Burgundian' clarity of flavours.
9. The Bier Library: Brew master Amit Mishra and owner Prashant Kunal rue India's love for Hefeweizens and Witbiers. Try the malty smoky German Rauchbocks, Belgian Dubbels, New England IPAs, and copper-coloured Altbiers. The inside-outside space is terrific for dinner, dancing, or checking emails like the techies do.
10. Toit: One of the earliest breweries in town, Toit took a beating in the middle because of its inconsistent brews. It remains popular for its buzz and red ale, which is arguably the best in town.
11. 7Rivers Brewing Co: Master brewer Lynette Pires has worked in other Bangalore outlets and creates a superb American Pale Ale. Located inside Taj MG Road, this brewery's central al fresco location makes it a favourite in the CBD (Central Business District).
12. Bira 91 Taproom: These guys are masters of innovation, launching new and seemingly crazy beers every week. People talk about their gin-infused beer with a tinge of ginger—sounds weird but tastes terrific. They launch

a new beer a week including Yuzu sours, pineapple sours, dragon fruit ales. Based on feedback, they decide on whether to bottle.

13. Arbor Brewing Co.: Brew master Arjun Tale brings his balanced sensibility towards signature brews such as the Beach Shack IPA, Raging Elephant—an ale that clocks in at 80 IBUs (International Bitterness Units) but which is actually very creamy and malty in the mouth. One of the earliest breweries, its central Bangalore location is a plus.
14. Windmills Craftworks: Relative to the others, this one is priced high. You go for the ambience. While their Spectrum IPA is well-regarded, most go for the whole package: good music, food and decent craft beer.
15. Buying beer in cans, bottles or crowlers: Go to Tonique, Drops, Madhuloka, or, if all else fails, Dewars—which can procure anything for you given time.

Final tip: Wines have sommeliers to recommend them. Talk to brew masters and owners when you go to craft breweries. You won't be sorry.

Gin trails and sensory trails in Bangalore's wine community

A few weeks ago, I organized a blind-tasting of nine pinot noirs from all over the world. I collected bottles of pinot noirs from France, where the grape originated, Italy, Germany, and Austria (which comprise the 'old world' wine regions, basically Europe), and then the 'new world' wine regions of Argentina, Chile, USA, Australia and New Zealand. All were the same vintage, 2019. The question was whether The Wine Connoisseurs or TWC, a wine group that I am part of, could rate all these wines based on what we liked and disliked. Secondly, whether we could even guess what the wines were without a label to guide us.

Here's what happened. Even though I had bought the bottles, and knew the names of the wines, I decided to attempt it blind. I sent the bottles to The Park Bengaluru where the event was held and told them to wrap up all the bottles and pour the wines into glasses labelled 1 to 9. As a result, each of us ten participants at the dinner were confronted with nine glasses of wine arranged in front of us. They all looked red and smelled, well, like wine. How to rate them according to our liking from 1 to 9? Like a student confronted with an exam paper, I froze. All the research I had done about wine regions and what a pinot noir wine smells like flew out of the window. For the record, although there are regional variations, the words used to describe the smell of the pinot noir grape are: cherries, cranberry, forest floor, mushrooms, smoke, licorice, tobacco, spicy and savoury notes. I swirled and sniffed with all my might but could not smell all this. All my preparation added up to nothing. How then to smell better? How then to remember what you smell? And how to translate this into practice?

Smell or olfaction is among the most ancient of our senses. In order to smell better, it seems obvious that you have to practise smelling. Children do this. My daughter, aged 10, used to walk into a room and say things like, 'Why does it smell like inside a temple?' Her references to smell were very specific and based on memory. As adults, we forget to smell. And now, it seems, we have to learn to smell everything: coffee, chocolate, gin, and, of course, wine. Every new brand is talking about the smells of their product. How was I going to get back this skill? By smelling every day, I guess. In India, this is easy. We are surrounded by smells but have stopped paying attention to them.

Gin and tequila are the spirits of the moment in Bangalore. For me, it is easy to spot Mezcal, given its smokiness. Tequila is almost impossible and has no smell. Gin is one of those spirits that is infused with smells. Recently, Kumaon-based Himmaleh Spirits showcased their new gins in Bangalore. What I liked about their flagship Kumaon & I gin were the facts that women farmed their grain, the bottle design was based on the hand-painted *aipan* art (something like rangoli) that Kumaon folks paint on their walls, and the botanicals were all local. Heard of black turmeric, peppery timur, or citrusy galgal? These are things I have never smelled, and these are the flavours that infuse these gins. Try as I might, I couldn't crack their individual olfaction, although when I mixed a gin and tonic, it had flavours of Himalayan juniper, and what we wine folks call a terrific mouthfeel. Their sister gin, called Jin-jiji and made with flavours of Darjeeling tea, is easier to spot. All of which leads to the question: how do you code scent memory in your head—through the familiar or the new?

We live in a society where looking and sight have taken precedence over every other sense. Sure, we hear traffic sounds, and bird calls, but particularly in large Indian cities we have learned to tune out sounds and smells. Yet, learning to smell is key if you are interested in food and drink. As James McHugh says in his book *Sandalwood and Carrion: Smell in Indian Religion and Culture,* our ancestors had a much greater tolerance for the spectrum of sense and smells that they encountered in everyday life. Categorizing them into good and bad smells is a modern problem.

Smell is a muscle that has to be cultivated continuously. Just like you can't expect to climb a mountain unless you climb every day, you can't expect to face wines or chocolate or gin, and be able to articulate what you smell unless you practise. The next time you go in your car, for example, put away that smart phone, open the window—this is Bangalore and so this is possible—and close your eyes, and smell. You will be amazed at the variety of scents that flow through our streets, or maybe you won't.

Bangalore savours the final flavours of mango season

Come July, and we mourn the mangoes. They are fading across India and also here in Bangalore. The mango stalls that pop up like a golden streak on Jayamahal Road are slowly winding down—packing up. Delhi, meanwhile, is smartly hosting the International Mango Festival just about now, an annual event since 1987, that has claimed this King of Fruits in all its glory. India, after all, is the world's largest producer of mangoes, contributing to a whopping 40 per cent of global production. We also are the world's largest exporter, sending over a million tonnes to the US, UK, UAE and everywhere else. But for Indians, the mango is more than a fruit. It is a reason to return home. It is a collective memory; a personal narrative and a common one. Here for example is my fanciful and imaginary primer on how to eat a mango, written from the point of view of a seven-year-old boy. Let's call him Kesar. I hope this resonates with each of you.

'Hello, I am Kesar, age 7, from a family of mango

growers. And here are my thoughts about mangoes.

'To eat a mango, you pull its cheeks, like old aunties do, before asking, at weddings, "Do you know who I am?", when all they are to you is plump, like an Alphonso mango. But mostly you don't understand why your parents cover your eyes and ears at the movies during the parts when the hero whispers that his lover's breasts are like ripe Dasheri mangoes. At seven years of age, your sexuality is utterly un-self-conscious and full of curiosity. You have forgotten how to suckle and you don't know yet what sucking means. Yet, you have to do both to your favourite variety, the Langda which your Dadu (grandfather) says you have to literally suck out. So you do. You purse your lips into what your teenage cousins call the "fish-face" as they pose for Instagram selfies. To you, a boy named after the golden Kesar mango, these fish-face poses look like those totem smiles on the Mayan picture books that you colour during summer holidays.

'Your mother meanwhile calls you Sakkara Kutty or Sugar Baby. But this mango is not one that you like. Sure, it smells good and is tiny enough to hold in your small hands, but the seed is large and the sugar is minimal. So, you sit in a corner of your large joint-family home and colour comics until your elder cousins, the boys you adore and worship, whisper that they are going out to get mangoes. In the midst of the afternoon as the family takes a siesta, you and your cousins escape to the Chausa orchards nearby to climb up trees and grab raw mangoes. The best variety for eating raw in your tiny opinion is the Neelam, which looks blue rather than green. Once, during such an afternoon jaunt, an elder cousin discovered an effigy at the foot of your Dadu's favourite Malgova mango tree. Inside the earth was buried an effigy: a tiny human figure made with paper and straw, with needles stuck on the spine. Slightly scared and very confused, you carried the tiny figure to your youngest uncle, whose face became as white as the inside of a Totapuri or parrot-beaked mango when he saw the figure. In whispered voices, your uncles conferred over the effigy and cursed fluently. Their Mallika crops were under siege, they said, by jealous neighbours who were doing black magic. When they see the fear in your innocent big eyes, your uncles hand you a Bainganapalli or Benishan mango. They instruct you to chew its beige flesh till juices drip into fake mustache stains on your brown face. Once you finish eating, you try to take out the mango fibres that flail between your teeth, awaiting your mother's determined toothbrush.

'On the fifth day of spring, the young women in your village wear mango-leaf crowns and yellow shimmering robes as they swing from hastily tied ropes wrapped with garlands and leaves. They swing over rivers, kicking swelling droplets on their amorous suitors. Every drupe, which is what a mango is (and I studied this in science class just so you know), dupes, by promising size when it is mostly seed. And so, this is Kesar, age 7, student at Army Public School, signing off.'

Now that you folks have read my fanciful essay on mangoes, it is time to get down to the business of mango pickling. As summer winds down, Bangalore's markets showcase late-season gems like Neelam and Mallika, bidding farewell to the mango fiesta. Those who were smart enough to snag some tiny pickling mangoes pull them out to marinate them in salt and chilli powder. The pickles will hopefully be ready next month to eat in time for Ganesh Chaturthi, which is when we will pull out mango leaves anyhow.

On that auspicious date, thousands of people carrying fruits, mango leaves and flowers will come with their clay Ganesha idols to offer to Bangalore's lakes. The idols will be ceremoniously taken through town in tractors and trucks before immolation. Perhaps we should revive our ancient animistic roots where nature was full of divinities; where the mango tree along with the sacred peepul was worshipped. After all, if we view our trees and lakes as divine, we will protect and cherish them in this land that Kempe Gowda founded. As his mother said, 'Plant trees, build lakes.' To that, I would add 'eat mangoes'.

Arts and Culture

From jaatres to pallakis: Bangalore's street fairs, floats and processions

Last week, I went to Vidhana Soudha for the first time after Covid. The occasion was 'Namma Jaatre', put forth by the Department of Kannada and Culture along with Kadambari Trust, founded by Chandra Jain. Flagged off by Chief Minister Siddaramaiah and Minister Shivaraj S. Tangadagi, it was a way to see the spectacular village fairs held all over the state—except we were in the heart of Bangalore. 'This really is a celebration of the Indian ecosystem where each village and each community has its own vibrant culture but the values that connect them are universal,' said Jain, who was intimately involved in organizing the fair.

And what a spectacle it was. First came the elephant Lakshmi, who blessed the dignitaries who stood on the dais and showered her with flowers. Then came a *rath* or chariot, followed by the state goddess Bhuvaneshwari on a flower-float, or *poo-pallaki* as they are called here. Then came a variety of folk artists, each with a different costume, dance and instruments. The *dollu kunitha,* for instance, are drummers; the *veeragase* men wear fabulous bronze snake-crowns, red attire and dance in warlike movements; the *yakshagana* artists had painted faces and dramatic headgear; the *karaga* dancers balanced pots and other objects on their head as they danced; the *kombu kahale* are curved musical instruments that were played before battle to spur the warriors—like a bugle; the *ettina gadi* is our bullock cart, except these ones were beautifully decorated; the *huli vesha* dancers are painted like tigers and engage in lithe movements; the *lambadi* or *lambani* dancers belong to the Banjara tribe and wear colourful handmade costumes and veils; the *goravara kunitha* are men who wear bear-hair on their heads; the *somanna kunitha* performers cover their faces in painted doll-masks; the *jagalige* drummers beat in unison; the *pooja kunitha* had male-female couple dancers; the *bisu kamsale* had male dancers with striped sacred marks on their foreheads, carrying a cymbal and a bronze disc to clang and beat while dancing.

Jain talked about the clash of cultures even within a state. For example, she said, the *goravara kunitha* performers usually wear hats made of bear-hair. Now, they were discouraged from doing this by 'animal protection people', even though their hats were made using dead bear skin and hair. 'They are so proud of their traditions, so connected to the earth. They are the ones who really take care of the environment. Now, we from the city are interfering and imposing our view on them without any understanding of their ecosystem,' said Jain.

Karnataka, like many Indian states, has over 1,000 village

fairs that take place throughout the year. Most are linked to seasons or festivals. Bangalore is a miniature in this area and has a whole host of fairs that happen within the city. They go by many names. *Jaatre* is the Kannada word for mela or fair. There are poo-pallakis or flower-floats that take place in different areas from September through December. There are fire-walking festivals, routine street processions that honour the rebuilding or opening of a local temple or church. Then, there are annual festivals like the St. Mary's Feast in Shivaji Nagar where millions of people gather on the streets for the procession.

During the Namma Jaatre festival, all the folk artists made their way from Vidhana Soudha to the Ravindra Kalakshetra where they set up stalls and showcased their art. There were stalls selling the intricate *kasuti* embroidery sarees from Upper Karnataka, and *bidri* work with its distinct black and silver appearance; leather puppets with their images of Rama, Sita, Ravana and other mythical figures; beautiful grain/rice *thorans* that people hang on their doors to feed birds, and *vetiver* roots that cooled the water kept in terracotta pots; specially designed *mangalsutra* bangles that had gold laid on glass; brightly coloured *ilkal* sarees with their distinct arrow-like borders. Since the whole thing was held in the Ravindra Kalakshetra with its spacious corridors and banyan tree courtyards, all the artists felt at home—performing, selling, and napping under the banyan trees.

All this is poignant because in the three months since the prime minister announced his Vishwakarma scheme, over 21 lakh applications were received from basket weavers, carpenters, tailors, masons and more.

The largest number of applications came from Karnataka state followed by West Bengal, which is known for its handwork. The fact that there are so many artisans and craftspeople here in Karnataka who have sought help from the PM's Vishwakarma scheme tells us about the richness of handwork available in this state, and also that it needs help.

Ravindra Kalakshetra is one of those little-known spaces in town. It is a great place to witness things that are quintessentially part of Kannada culture—puppet shows, dance performances, Kannada theatre and craft fairs. The pity is that not many people know about it and there is no easy way to find out what is happening there on a regular basis. They don't have a social media page or a mailing list. The best way I know is to go on 'Book My Show' and insert Ravindra Kalakshetra as the venue. Today I did that and found a lively roster of Kannada plays that were happening this week and next.

Go visit. Who knows? You may find a street fair happening in the process.

When Ganesha gets a six-pack: Pandal hopping in Bangalore

Of course, Mumbai is the city that is associated with Vinayaka, Ganesha, Ganapathy, call him what you will. But if you are in Bangalore this weekend—the weekend after Ganesh Chaturthi, you may be surprised to find that this city can provide spirited competition in the spectacle area.

I have just returned from spending a few hours going from 'pandal' to 'pandal', each dedicated to Lord Ganesha. One has him dressed as Shiva, complete with blue skin, half-moon on matted hair and trident in hand. Another giant Ganesha has a ball coming out of his trunk and a cricket bat in his hand. A third has him ride a tiger à la Durga. The fourth has him with a dozen hands, each holding a different weapon. My favourite though is Ganesha in padmasana, sporting a six-pack, almost as if he has ditched the modaks for a workout. To see all this, you need to drive to Ulsoor Lake on the night of the visarjan, which this year is on the Sunday following Ganesh Chaturthi, in this instance the 15th—which happens to be Onam as well, which means that there will be flowers on the floor and processions on the road.

The Ganesha visarjan, which is the immersion of the Ganesha idols into water, happens in Ulsoor Lake in North Bangalore. About 100 Ganesha idols of all sizes and shapes will arrive on lorries, tractors and cranes, with loud music and dance. While India's festivals are all glorious and grand, this particular festival is dear to many, mostly because of the community participation—much like Durga Puja in Kolkata. Diwali is largely done at home, Navarathri tends to be largely dominated by ladies, small festivals like Sankranti and Basant Panchami are regional, Holi is terrific but really a North Indian festival, and so it goes. Ganesha somehow is a pan-Indian inclusive and communal festival. Or so I thought, as I drove down Tannery Road, only to come across huge crowds of police officers literally all along the road. There were buses with reserve forces, waterjets to control crowds, lathi-wielding security guards and plain-clothes officers. In a historical irony that has become a current nightmare, the procession of this overtly Hindu God takes place through a densely populated Muslim area. No wonder, the shops were shuttered and the roads were bare. A few burqa-clad women walked through the streets, but largely it was groups of men and boys with red vermillion streaked across their foreheads, decorating the tree-sized Ganesha with garlands in preparation for the procession. There was 'annadana', or food, being served to the community. But the police presence reminded me that this festival which glorifies the elephant-God has also, in the past, resulted in Hindu-Muslim riots. I talked to residents in the area who recounted one event a few years ago when a Muslim threw a stone and broke off one of the arms of Ganesha. A furious Hindu mob apparently chopped off a pig's head and laid it inside a mosque, following which they ransacked Muslim shops and homes.

The area where I live in North Bangalore is a hotbed of communal tension because it has a strong Muslim, Christian and Hindu population. While this is fine on a normal day, festivals make the whole street and situation an 'India-Pakistan' affair, as one resident said. Hence the huge police presence on this stretch of road.

What were the highlights of my four hours on the street with Ganesha? The spirited Ramraj band doing a drum-jam in front of a purple Shiva-Ganesha. A group of young boys dancing to 'Naatu Naatu' in front of my six-pack Ganesha. A dignified old lady standing behind a giant cauldron of delicious vegetarian pulao and amazing onion-raita, filling paper plates with food and handing over to me (and a line of others). Little girls in pink frocks taking selfies in front of a psychedelically lit Ganesha. A kitten sat beside a gun-toting policeman and he fed it some milk. A framed and garlanded photo of Puneeth Rajkumar next to a Ganesha, showing once again how he was an actor of the people. Ganesha on an autorickshaw with a burqa-clad lady taking a photo of him. But these are the happy images. There are haunting ones as well—of bearded Muslim shopkeepers standing in front of shuttered shops and watching this giant procession of an elephant-God who has made them lose business on this particular day. So yes, Indian festivals are glorious but that also depends on which festival and who you ask.

What is wonderful though is the spectacle of it and the way the image has been interpreted in imaginative ways. As I came back home, I noticed lines of people—men, women and children—sitting at their door, drinking chai, and getting ready to watch colour, music and dance for the next hour as a line of Ganeshas went by in a procession to be immersed into Ulsoor Lake.

∞

From the ghats to the gallery: Karnataka's folk arts and forests

When I first moved to Bangalore nearly 20 years ago, I didn't know that Karnataka as a state was only named in 1973, thanks to the efforts of then Chief Minister Devaraj Urs (or Arasu) along with eminent Kannadigas like Kuvempu, Shivarama Karanth, Masti Venkatesha Iyengar, A.N. Krishna Rao, B.M. Srikantaiah, D.V. Gundappa, K.V. Puttappa, and many others who together realized the dream of Aluru Venkata Rao, who began the Kannada Ekikarana (unified purpose) movement as early as 1905.

Karnataka Rajyotsava, celebrated each year on 1 November, is a great time to be in Bangalore. It is a time when Karnataka's folk arts are on display and what a spectacle it is. Venues throughout the city will organize exhibitions and workshops on Karnataka's cultural traditions, and crafts like Chittara Art, Kasuti embroidery, or Siddhi quilt making. There will also be performances such as Dollu Kunitha drums, and Carnatic music. After all, this is the land that gave its name to that music tradition.

The other places to enjoy Karnataka's unique offerings during the Rajyotsava week and month are Rangashankara, where a number of excellent Kannada plays will take place, and Chitrakala Parishath where exhibitions of Karnataka art will take place. A few years ago, I attended one where Nicolas Roerich's painting were exhibited at CKP or Chitra Kala Parishath. The Roerich estate is vast and lies on the outskirts of Bangalore. It was owned by Nicholas's late son, Svetoslav, and Svetoslav's late wife, film actress Devika Rani. As birdwatchers, we always used to hanker after entering the estate, but it was closed to the public for years. Instead, the nature community goes to other places in South Bangalore including the Bannerghatta National Park.

The first week of November also marks the International Day for Biosphere Reserves, on the 3rd. Perhaps because of Bangalore's location, the magnificent Nilgiri Biosphere Reserve and the Western Ghats are accessible to us. Is it this proximity that makes so many Bangaloreans passionate nature lovers and also filmmakers? Recently, Rohini Nilekani Philanthropies and Felis Films released a trailer of their upcoming documentary on the Nilgiris with terrific footage of the land and people who live in, and love, these Blue Mountains. I was born in Coimbatore. Every summer, my family and I would take the Nilgiri Express or the Blue Mountain Express to go visit my grandparents. Ooty and Coonoor, now occupied by some of Bangalore's super-rich, used to be our summer stomping ground. It was on these school trips to the Nilgiris that I learned about nature conservation.

There are two camps when it comes to nature

conservation and neither can understand the other. Conservationists will stake their principles and sometimes their life to save something that they deem important, be it a grassland or a species. The other camp does not understand why saving the spotted owl (or turtles, bears or butterflies) is so important when you could be building toilets or reducing poverty. Of course, you can do both—save nature and humans. But often, when it comes to nature conservation, humans are the villains. Occasionally, they become saviours too, which is where this story begins.

Recently, the Karnataka government approved a proposal that would create a 5,010-acre sanctuary for migrating birds, small mammals and countless insects. Named the Greater Hesaraghatta Conservation Reserve (GHCR), the approval order was met with relief from conservationists such as Mahesh Bhat, Seshadri K.S. and the late Ramki Sreenivasan, who had petitioned for this for over a decade.

I learned about this when I visited Hesaraghatta a month ago. It was part of the weekend birdwatching 'outings' organized by Bangalore Birds. Every Sunday, for many years, the group organizes nature walks in different parts of the city, all of which are announced on their website: bngbirds.com. So if you are in Bengaluru one weekend and want to learn about nature, join the group. The first Sunday is Saul Kere (*kere* means 'lake' in Kannada), the second, at Lalbagh. The third Sunday used to be at Jakkur Lake, but the birdwatching community decided to move it to Hesaraghatta. The logic was that routine visits by birdwatchers would help monitor the grasslands that nature-lovers hold dear.

Conservation and communication are two sides of the same coin. Sometimes, conservationists team up with filmmakers (Ramki Sreenivasan and Shekar Dattatri are an example). For wildlife filmmakers, engaging with conservationists and the nature community is a way to stay rooted to the flora and fauna that they both love. For as long as I have known her, filmmaker Sugandhi Gadadhar, along with her husband Rana Belur, has been filming smooth-coated otters along the Kaveri river. Recently, I ran into Sugandhi at the Bangalore Bird Day and asked what she was up to. 'Still otters,' she replied with a smile. What she didn't say was that she was speaking at the prestigious Wildscreen Festival in the UK this year. Sandesh Kadur has done stellar work on the Sahyadris through his photos, books and films. He constantly talks about collaboration between wildlife filmmakers and conservationists to help a common cause.

The fact that Bangalore is blessed with both filmmakers and conservationists is perhaps why the wildlife conservation movement is thriving in this city.

Can Bengaluru become the next Goa for creatives?

I am deep within the woodlands of North Bangalore, where owls roost and eagles call. This evening though, the place is lit up with string lights and filled with music-lovers who are there to listen to a line-up of 40 or so Indian and international artists including Sid Sriram, 8Kays, Thaikkudam Bridge and many more. Not enough women artistes, is my quibble.

Echoes of Earth bills itself as 'India's greenest music festival', by bringing 'conservation into the conversation', according to festival director Roshan Netalkar. They do this by building the giant sets out of recycled waste materials and naming them after fantastic forest creatures—tusker, rhino beetle and serpent this year. Plastic is banned, RO water is everywhere—offered not in throwaway paper cups but stainless-steel glasses. Most importantly, each year the festival's theme celebrates nature. Last year the theme was 'circle of life'. This year, the theme 'ensemble of the earth' celebrates the Western Ghats. Roshan is from Karwar, so the Sahyadris are personal to him. 'The

Western Ghats take care of 40 per cent of our population, three rivers flow out from there, it is the world's eighth biggest biodiversity hotspot,' he reels off. Which brings him to his pet passion. 'How do you have a conversation with the younger generation about sustainability? Music is the answer,' he says.

Echoes of Earth festival, which began in Bangalore in 2016, has grown bigger every year. Next year though, and this is a sobering thought, the festival is going to Goa in February. What does Goa have that Bangalore doesn't, and why are so many creative types attracted to Goa? Let's not get into the richie-rich types who are buying up half of Goa. This piece is about land fostering a creative ferment and certain places do it better than others—Jaipur, Chennai, Pune and Goa come to mind. Can Bangalore aspire to be part of the mix?

What does it take for a city to catalyse creativity? Which are the global cities known to foster a creative ferment—like Florence did in the 15th century? In India, the only five cities to be mentioned in UNESCO's list of Creative Cities are Srinagar and Jaipur for crafts, Chennai and Varanasi for music, Mumbai for film, and Hyderabad for gastronomy. Goa would not have qualified because it is not a city, but mention the creative life to any Indian and most of us will point to Goa.

In order for creativity to flourish, there needs to be two things: a community of interested patrons and a congregation of artists that can create a trickle-down effect through students. Bangalore, so far, has had neither. Our city has been so caught up in commerce and enterprise that we have been busy creating start-ups, which is great for the city's economy, but not necessarily for that intangible thing we call culture.

A few organizations are trying to change Bangalore's identity with respect to the arts. This year, for instance, marks the first year of what is perceived to be an annual festival celebrating Bangalore in all its glory—including the arts, nature, performances, history and walks. Called Unboxing Bangalore Habba (Habba means festival), the festival on-boards as many interested 'partners' as possible. In that sense, it is not a patronage model, but rather a platform model. Individual organizations who are part of the Habba create 'properties' such as nature tours, dance performances, museum walks and book readings that will attract—hopefully—a new audience. Running from December 1–11 this year, the Habba hopes to become bigger each year, attracting people from all over India and abroad, much like the Chennai December Music Festival has done.

The Bangalore Literature Festival which just concluded remains community-funded and grows bigger every year.

What all these festivals have in common is the ability to bring a large group of people together around a theme. Post-Covid, nobody wants to do virtual events. We all enjoy face-to-face interactions that include eye contact and touch. What happens in such congregations is that you run into people you know well or slightly. Conversations happen, spawning ideas and hopefully these ideas get taken further into the creation of something. This is what happened in Athens around the time of Socrates, in Varanasi in the 8th century when all the Sanskrit poets and scholars made their way there, and in Chennai today, when musicians who grow up in the US—like Sid Sriram—make their home in Mylapore, Chennai.

Bangalore does not—as of today at least—attract artists, be they performers, writers or visual designers. Artists who make their home here have other links—family, weather, spousal job, grew up here. The majority don't *seek* out Bangalore as a place where their creative art will flourish. Is this changeable and will Bangalore be able to pull it off?

I sure hope so, because you know what—it is all very well to be the start-up capital of India and chase money, but the best things in life are either priceless or free. Bangalore has just started realizing this. Now, it needs to take this realization into action.

Hubba happenings: Creating a festival of festivals in Bengaluru

Open the BLR Hubba homepage (https://blrhubba.in/) and I guarantee that you are going to get overwhelmed by the number of things on offer. Currently in its second edition with a budget of ₹8 crore, the Hubba runs from November 30 to December 14 at different venues across Bangalore. They have received flak over the spelling of the word 'Hubba', as opposed to the more common Habba. But the fact remains that this ambitious effort, helmed and facilitated by a group of passionate Bangaloreans, is trying to put Bangalore on the national and international cultural map. One can count 16 days, 500+ events, 40 locations. We are no longer just an IT city. That's the hope anyway. Which brings up the first question: Is the Hubba trying to be all things to all people? The short answer from chief facilitator V. Ravichandar is an unapologetic yes. For Ravi, the self-described 'patron saint of lost causes', the Hubba needs to educate and entertain all Bangaloreans, no matter where they live or who they are. Hence the more-is-more approach.

There are some verticals. Live music (named Kantha) happens in the evening at Freedom Park, with artistes including Pashabhai, M.D. Pallavi, the Bangalore Children's Chorus and other performers from across India. Gode or Wall incorporates street art murals by a variety of artists across different metro stations of Bangalore. Chosen through an open call by a respected jury of art practitioners including Suresh Jayaram, Archana Hande and Ravikumar Kashi, GodeBLR is curated by Kamini Sawhney. The performing art series, titled Offbeat, has a number of collaborations. Guru-Shishya as evident by the name includes performances by respected teachers and their senior students including stalwarts such as Vinayak Torvi, M.S. Sheela, Poornima Kulkarni and many others. There are also performances in beautiful heritage city spaces such as Panchavati, the home of Sir C.V. Raman in Malleshwaram, and Sabha, a new theatre space on Kamaraj Road. A Maker's Trail, which highlights collaboration between architecture and design, curated by Manju Sara Rajan, is a way to go behind the scenes.

Kannada music, dance and theatre take centre stage in Gala Gala Gaddala—talk about a name that doesn't take itself seriously. Curated by Lekha Naidu, the series has plays, ganevadya which is a mixture of music, poetry and storytelling in Kannada, music and puppet-based performances at different venues. There are also street markets all over the city on weekends where artisans and performers take over neighbourhoods to showcase their wares and talent. Speaklore spans the spectrum of spoken-word performances ranging from Harikatha and

Kerala's puppet play to improv jam and spoken-word poetry. Futures is a conversation about the future of journalism and history by experts.

So how to make sense of this? My approach is to choose a space/venue near where you live and attend performances there. The other way is to choose one or two highlight events that you have been wanting to see and try to catch these select events. Putting an umbrella over multiple happenings in the city including the Bangalore Literature Festival is what this Hubba excels at.

Meanwhile, the Karunada Habba, arguably more egalitarian and inclusive, is going to happen in Jayanagar 5th Block, Shalini Grounds, from 29 November through 1 December. Finding information about it online is hard—I got the details only through Whatsapp forwards. There are cooking, rangoli, music, painting, group dance, solo dance and singing competition, all in Kannada, with cash prizes. Sponsored by News 18, this Habba makes its way from Hospet and Shivamogga to Bangalore.

The Museum of Art and Photography (MAP) holds its annual Art is Life festival on 30 November and 1 December. There are workshops, screenings, guided walks and special performances.

After a long day at work, why should you attend any of these Habbas or festivals? Unlike watching TV alone at home, being with people is mood-enhancing. Research proves that we humans are social animals and like being around others in our tribe. Engaging with live performances also triggers the mirror neurons in our brain, causing pleasurable and relaxing sensations. I find that live performances are also great for generating ideas because you are in a meditative state of relaxed awareness. So carry your notebook, journal, or sketchbook; forget your smartphone for a few minutes and delve into the rich treasures of music, art and culture that are so bountifully available this December in Bangalore. You will not regret it.

When will a Kannadiga character appear in Bollywood?

When I saw *Rocky Aur Rani Kii Prem Kahaani*, the thought occurred: when will a Kannadiga character populate a mainstream Bollywood movie? *Rocky Rani* has the Bengali Chatterjees. *Chennai Express* has Tamilians. Why are there no Kannadiga characters in mainstream movies? Is it because they don't inspire the popular imagination? Is it because they don't have strong traits that can be caricatured, like the 'intellectual Bengalis' or the 'flashy Punjabis'? What are the signature traits of the Kannadigas?

There are two, and neither will help with getting us into Bollywood. Ask the outsiders who have populated Bangalore about Kannadigas, and a few adjectives come out. One is that Kannadigas have a 'softness' to them. They are gentle, genteel, civilized. How to portray this in a Bollywood potboiler? But politeness is not the only trait that marks Kannadigas or Bangaloreans. What is interesting is that two of Instagram's most popular comics are based in this city: Ayyo Shraddha and Danish Sait.

Both portray layered aspects of life in Bangalore. They are snarky, sarcastic, rude, jumpy, silly and more. Why are these qualities not capturing the imagination of popular and mainstream cinema?

In general, Karnataka is not good at marketing. The world knows Kanjivaram sarees but who has heard of Molkalmuru silks from our state? This state is at the crossroads of Hindustani and Carnatic music but somehow the world associates Chennai with music. Some part of our poor marketing has to do with branding. Most people associate places or products with just one or at most two adjectives. Bangalore, and for that matter Karnataka, perhaps has too many layers. Our state slogan, 'One State Many Worlds', is both accurate and confusing because it does not tell us what those 'worlds' are. In contrast, Kerala's 'God's Own Country' branding evokes poetic visuals in our minds. Cities too need a strong personality for them to stand out, like Mumbai did in the *Munna Bhai* movies. We Bangaloreans may think that our city has a strong personality but clearly, Bollywood doesn't know what that is.

Of course, this brings up the whole question of whether you would want a Kannadiga character in a Bollywood film. As my intellectual (naturally) Bengali friend said, 'Bollywood reduces characters to caricatures. Why would you wish for that?' Because it is a marker of having arrived in the national conscious—just like India bidding for the 2036 Olympics is a measure of the nation's confidence, its belief of having arrived on the global scene.

In Bangalore, the tech, IT and start-up worlds take up all the air space. There is little room for much else.

You would think that a Bollywood film with edgy, crazy, twisted characters that are creating a start-up would make for lots of drama (backstabbing, name-dropping, insecure egos, betrayal, it's all there), but that hasn't happened. The closest we have come to is in the stand-up comedy world, where Bangalore has been the runway for many including 'Pushpavalli', 'Ayyo Shradda' and Danish Sait.

So, what will it take for Bangalore to catch the national imagination? First of all, Bangaloreans have to make it to the top of creative industries. The reason so many Bollywood movies are based on Punjabi families is because many of the film producers are from that state. Many of the music conductors are from Bengal. Producers talk to musicians and creative cross-pollination happens. A character is born. Bangaloreans are mostly in IT, not Bollywood. This is not a value judgement. Economic prosperity comes before the thriving of culture. Tokyo became a financial powerhouse in the 80s before it became known globally for fashion brands like Sacai, designers like Takashi Murakami and Yayoi Kusama.

I believe that this is the inflection point for Bangalore to take off in areas that go beyond tech. Museums are being built in our city. Lots of books based on Bangalore are being published. It is sad that one of the slick podcasts that is made in Bangalore is 'WTF with Nikhil Kamath', where he talks in an echo chamber made up of his buddies who are all in—no surprise there—tech.

The soft power that comes from Korean television serials, its music and fashion is a long way off for Bangalore because like it or not, we are still a city with a programming, engineering mindset that values dot.coms more than connecting the dots in a creative-imaginative fashion. Cultural cross-pollination can only happen if culture is celebrated, which it is not in Bangalore. Until that happens, Bangalore will still be stuck in a linear mindset that is about dollars and cents rather than larger-than-life personalities who capture the popular imagination.

❧

Shakti in Shivaji Nagar: Bangalore's tribal fierce goddesses

As a woman, one of the things that I fight against is the weight of expectation that family, society and culture puts on me. I hate it. At least within the family, I can and have pushed back. I have told my mother and mother-in-law that I cannot be like them: light the lamp every day, cook food for the family (I am a horrible cook), and play by the rules. My husband, of course, gets the brunt of all my outbursts. Society, too, is adapting to new norms for women. I wasn't allowed to wear shorts outside when I grew up in Chennai. Today in Bangalore, you can walk down the bazaar street in Vasanth Nagar where Pavithra Condiments, Shree Raja fruit juice centre, and Parameshwari provision store exist. To my pleasant surprise, girls were sauntering down the street in shorts to buy and eat pani puri on the street. The weight of cultural expectations, though, is hard to dislodge. I blame it on the Hindu goddesses who loom large in the Indic imagination. They are thought of as 'mothers', givers of prosperity like Lakshmi, and the Sita who accepts everything. What happened to the fierce goddesses like Kali, who could give us permission to invoke the warrior within us? Well, let me tell you what happened. They went underground.

I am in a tiny home deep within the recesses of Shivaji Nagar. Behind a curtain is a man who is being dressed in a purple saree. He wears red lipstick and a big bindi. In a few hours, he will become a goddess.

The goddess enters him on new moon nights typically, called Amavasya in Hinduism. It is a day of austerity and for some, fasting. When this happens, Bala-anna (Anna means elder brother in many South Indian languages), as he is known, goes into a trance. He allows the goddess, Angala Parameshwari, to inhabit his body fully. He celebrates her. He dons his best saree and receives a steady stream of devotees. They come to see him, but really, they come to see her: the fierce tribal goddess who fixes all problems. Through her, Bala becomes soothsayer and savant, guru and goddess, counsellor and cushion—for their life's issues. Bala is an anomaly. He doesn't identify himself as gay or transgender. He is a man who the goddess visits. That is his firm belief. When I asked him about religion, he says that he worships snake gods and fierce goddesses like Muthyalamma, Nagamma and Angalamma. Later that night, when the goddess fully inhabits him, Bala bends over a pile of meat and stuffs it into his mouth. He throws the meat over his devotees as prasadam. He walks on fire, quite literally, leading a bunch of girls who participate in the fire-walking ceremony. It is spectacular to watch.

As an Indian woman brought up with the expectation that women are the keepers of harmony within family and community, I find these fierce goddesses liberating. The problem is that most of us have forgotten them. Think of Chinnamasta, one of the ten Mahavidyas. She is nude, stands on a copulating couple, cuts off her own head, and holds her severed head in one of her hands. Three jets of blood spurt out of her neck: one jet of blood is drunk by her severed head, and the other two by her two female attenders. As fierce feminine imagery, it is as powerful as it can get. Could women who had been trained to be people-pleasers benefit from this goddess's image? I believe so.

The sacred and the profane are not separate in India. They are braided together in everyday objects and life. The majestic bar-headed goose which is the vehicle of Saraswati, the goddess of learning, becomes a hamsa-motif that is woven into our textiles and sarees. The tree of life is drawn on the walls of rural homes. Icons and ideas from nature and religion are part of temple architecture, Vedic astrology, jewellery motifs, textile designs, and the rich repository of Hindu myths and fairy tales. As a practising Hindu, I use mandalas, mantras and rituals to access the soul and the spirit. Simultaneously as someone who studies and practises Carl Jung's depth psychology, I use the symbols and images of my dreams to access my unconscious. I would like to connect Hindu mythology with its rich and fantastic array of mystical symbols with the Jungian psychology that I practise in a way that will shed new light on two old practices. With the current crises in mental health all over the world including India, psychology has become an essential component by which we cope with the world. To my mind, combining the psychology that I learned with the Hindu faith that I inherited seem very natural. That doesn't mean it is easy. There is no blueprint because each dream is different. Connecting our inner lives to our collective myths is an exercise in poetic thinking.

So here I am, chewing on some cake—in preparation for Christmas, drinking some mulled wine, and listening to the Harlem Boys Choir take me to the next big festival in the Indian calendar.

Theatre in Bengaluru: Rangashankara to rooftop plays

Even growing up in insular Chennai in the 80s, I had heard of Marathi street theatre that went on all night. Tamil Nadu, too, had its 'theru-koothu', which means street-play, but my mother did not allow me to go out and watch them all night like my male cousins did—a sore spot for a spirited girl. Karnataka, like every other Indian state, also has a robust night life beyond the pubs and nightclubs which includes theatre, music performances, and processions, all of which are linked to religious institutions. For example, the chariot processions, or 'ther', linked to St. Mary's Feast brings Shivaji Nagar to a halt. This includes live music and dancing but not necessarily theatre. Live theatre (either on the street or on stage) is hard to access, at least for me in Central Bangalore. Imagine my delight when I came upon a Kannada play called 'Shivadoota Guliga', thanks to a popular app-cum-Whatsapp group called Putting Scene, which compiles cultural and culinary activities that happen in Bangalore every week. If you want to know what's happening beyond the usual stand-up stuff, get on the Putting Scene Whatsapp group.

Shivadoota Guliga staged at Ravindra Kalakshetra is a surreal and phantasmagorical Kannada musical-play which talks about the spirit-gods that roam around Tulu Nādu. *Kantara* the film made this famous but there are a host of 'bhoothas' or spirits that punish and protect the people here. The play is about how Guliga the Bhootha came down to earth. It had all the elements of the rich mythology that India is famous for. He came from the sweat of Shiva, was taken into the stomach of Vishnu, and was born to fulfil the curse of Brahma. A special scene is when Goddess Chamundi comes on stage, complete with ten hands and fireworks all around—it was a hit with the school children who packed the auditorium. Actor Swaraj Shetty—who played Guruva in *Kantara*—was in the lead role of the play written by Vijaykumar Kodialbail.

There are many eminent theatre personalities of the Kannada stage including Prasanna, B.V. Karanth and B. Jayashree. They were all products of the National School of Drama (NSD). Prasanna and Karanth went on to become directors of NSD. Jayashree (with Ananda Raju) started the group called Spandana, devoted to rediscovering the roots of Kannada theatre. Other stalwarts like B. Chandrasekhara (BC), C.R. Simha, B. Narayana (called Nani, who is current thespian Prakash Belawadi's father), S. Ramaswamy, Vimala Rangachar, S.G. Ramachandra, Suresh Heblikar, K.C. Shekar, and Upasane Seetharam were legendary contributors to both Kannada and English language theatre. I got all this information from Vijay Padaki, who founded Bangalore Little Theatre (BLT).

He had been on my mind because he won a Lifetime Achievement Award conferred by Assitej International (an organization of theatre professionals spread over 75 countries) in Havana, Cuba.

I asked Padaki what differentiated theatre in Karnataka as opposed to other Indian states. 'Karnataka stood out in one respect. We produced writers!' he replied. Kannada theatre had its golden period in the seventies when Kannada stage writing was creative and robust. English-language plays followed and have continued to this day. Several organizations including BLT worked on adaptations and translations to original scripts. In 2020, BLT launched a publications project. 'Ten volumes of plays are coming out of BLT. Plays are generally published by individuals. It is good for the CV. No theatre group has published plays under its name,' said Padaki.

Theatre is a great way to understand Bangalore. Both Ranga Shankara and Jagriti have a robust programme of Kannada plays, as does the Bangalore International Centre and Ravindra Kalakshetra. They also have summer theatre for young people which is essential to cultivate a taste for theatre. My daughter learned theatre with Kirtana Kumar, who, besides acting, has taught a generation of young people. Institutions like the Alliance Francaise and the Goethe Institute also support and champion theatre performances. Of course, there are stalwarts like the late great Girish Karnad who have become synonymous with acting and theatre.

That said, Kannada theatre is plagued by the same problems that theatre companies all over India, and perhaps the world, are dealing with. There is an ongoing struggle to survive, poor financial viability; a floating population of theatre artists who seek livelihoods elsewhere; poor public appreciation, with reliance on a loyalist constituency; founder-centric theatre companies and personality-dependent management; opportunistic programming, rather than strategic orientation; and so it goes. 'It is quite understandable, and to be looked at sympathetically,' said Padaki. 'This state of the theatre is because of pitiably low social investment. It makes us terribly preoccupied with the "success" of the single theatre organization, neglecting the development of the theatre as an institution.'

After watching the spate of plays that have been coming out in Bengaluru, I can only fervently hope that this state of affairs will change.

Brushes and beats: The artists who made Bangalore

Even though I have lived in Bangalore for nearly 20 years, there are certain parts of the city that are inaccessible to me, mostly because I did not grow up here. I feel this acutely because I have this understanding of nuance in Chennai where I was raised. In Chennai, I understand the meaning of silences and whether a certain look between two friends means that they are humouring you or mocking you. I know the voice tonalities and how to differentiate between sarcasm and suggestions in a way that I cannot do yet in Kannada. Hell, I even know the meaning of sighs in Chennai.

Usually, I don't feel this acutely in Bangalore because it is by and large a welcoming city, populated by immigrants who now call it home. But every now and then, I gain entry into the world of Kannadigas and I realize what I am missing. It is a connection with a people that only language and land can foster. You need to have lived in the land and speak its tongue.

Recently, the K.K. Hebbar Art Foundation along with

Manipal Institute of Art Education held a screening of a film on Hebbar's collaborations with Shivarama Karanth. The programme showed many aspects of Hebbar including his 'singing' line drawings. The film screening was followed by a live yakshagana programme called 'Kamsavadhe (killing of Kamsa)' by Begar Shivakumar, who founded the Gaana Sourabha Yakshagana School in Bangalore. D.A. Prasanna, who is married to Rajni, one of Hebbar's daughters, fronted and conceptualized the whole thing. Prasanna is an erudite scholar of Kannada history and pulled together multiple valences for the programme. I was sitting with Ullas Karanth, who besides being a formidable conservation biologist also happens to be the son of Shivarama Karanth. Also in the table were Chiranjeev Singh, the turban-clad former ambassador and bureaucrat who knows more about Kannada culture than most Kannadigas. Listening to them talk was a treat. Pratibha Karanth described how traditional yakshagana performances at their villages involved live handheld fire-sticks that were stoked by sawdust and how the 'rakshasas' or demons would run through the audience, scaring the children. Ullas talked about how the yakshagana costumes during his father's time were more subtle, subdued, and had a distinct aesthetic. On stage, Prasanna and Hebbar's daughters—Rajni and Rekha—talked about artistic collaborations that enlivened arts and literature. It was a feast for the senses.

Contrast Hebbar's line drawings with a recent exhibition held at Gallery G of Raja Ravi Varma's unseen paintings including one of Maharani Sethu Lakshmi Bayi as a three-year-old, painted by her grandfather, Raja

Ravi Varma. Gitanjali Maini, the founder of Gallery G, has roots in Kerala and connections with the Raja Ravi Varma Heritage Foundation. I grew up with lithographs of Raja Ravi Varma paintings—they are cherished images that adorn most puja rooms in Hindu homes in South India. But stylistically, Varma is more Rubens, and Hebbar is, well, minimalist in his line drawings. In his memoir, *Another Sort of Freedom*, writer Gurcharan Das talks about his philosophy of *laghima*, a Sanskrit word that connotes lightness of spirit; the ability to not take yourself too seriously. This lightness of spirit suffuses Hebbar's work.

Kynkyny art gallery is also one I follow because both its owners have strong roots to this land and have parlayed it in ways that create a positive ripple effect. Co-founder Vivek Radhakrishnan is Sir C.V. Raman's grandson. Namu Kini, his wife and co-founder, curates well-respected markets in Hatworks Boulevard, owned by Rishad Minochar (another old Bangalorean), which I enjoy. Recently, Paula Mariwala, my birding friend from Mumbai, pointed me to an exhibition in Kynkyny of Manish Chavda's art inspired by birds. More recently, Kynkyny created a stunning solo exhibit of Avijit Dutta which began with him creating a stamp commemorating C.V. Raman. Best of all, the exhibit was mounted in Panchavati, C.V. Raman's verdant home in Malleshwaram.

I love Karnataka artists—every single one of them. And there are many. There is Sheela Gowda's visceral and cerebral work; Ranjani Shettar's ethereal sculptures; Manjunath Kamath's jewel-like nests of art; N.S. Harsha's dreamy paintings and sculptures with girth—he is curating an interesting public art project for Kaash art gallery.

There is Pushpamala's dramatic self-portraits, which, to me, are more interesting than Cindy Sherman; Shanthamani, whose sculptural installations I had admired before I met her through her husband, the photographer Mallik Katakol; L.N. Tallur, whose darker works with skeletons and allusions to death I love; Prabhavati Meppayil, whose Avenue Road studio I have visited; S.G. Vasudev, who was the first artist I interviewed as a young college student—he was living in Cholamandalam then. He is now married to Ammu Joseph, who also went to Women's Christian College in Chennai—like me. Then there is the generous and understated sculptor, Balan Nambiar, who taught young kids art in a free Sunday class that he has held for years. Designer Sujata Keshavan once said that she attended his class, as did my kids.

Perhaps one of the best ways to access old and Kannadiga Bangalore is through its artists—past and present.

∞

Is Bangalore the hub of classical dance?

If you are visiting Bengaluru and want to see a classical music or dance performance, go to ADA Rangamandira theatre and (across the road from it) Ravindra Kalakshetra. Dance companies like this theatre because it is affordable to rent, relative to the larger Chowdiah Hall.

Bangalore is blessed with a multitude of classical dance forms relative to, say, nearby Chennai where Bharatanatyam reigns supreme, or Hyderabad where Kuchipudi takes pride of place. In Bangalore, you can find Kathak, Odissi, Bharatanatyam, Kuchipudi and other dance forms, all of which mesh together in this melting pot of a city. Why is not dance more popular than music? After all, through dance you can access all of India's classical art forms. There is music of course, whether Carnatic or Hindustani, that forms the background to the dance. There are India's rhythm forms, which form part of the beat of dance. There is aesthetics, revealed through costumes and make up. There is theatre, told through the stories depicted in the dance. There are stage sets, which let you access ancient Indian architecture and its idea of sacred spaces. If dance is such a complete package, how come there aren't more dance festivals in Bangalore, or for that matter, India?

I asked this question to Ramesh Swamy, who co-founded Unnati and Utsav. He and his team put together an annual Gokulashtami festival for Carnatic music at Odakathur Mutt in Ulsoor. How come you don't include more dance in your festival, I asked Ramesh, especially given that his son, Vhishal, is a dancer and part of the Aayana dance company. 'It is a catch-22,' says Ramesh. 'Part of the problem is that we don't have enough good auditoriums to host dance performances.' This year, he explains, they invited Mohiniattam dancers at the tail-end of the Gokulashtami festival. 'We couldn't even offer them a green room to get ready before the performance,' he says. 'Cost and sponsorship is the other issue.'

To put together a dance performance is more expensive than to have a singer and accompanists on stage. You need lights, technicians, a green room for getting dressed, and a stage large enough to hold an ensemble. In Bangalore—and perhaps this is the case in most Indian cities—such stages are hard to come by. Given this, most dance festivals are organized by dance gurus and dance schools, because they understand the technical needs of their art forms more than anyone else.

The Bangalore International Centre (BIC) stands in pleasant contrast to most other auditoriums or festivals because it has emerged as a patron of the performing arts and specifically dance. Recently, I watched an outstanding performance by the Natya Institute of Kathak & Choreography (disclosure: I serve on its board) at the BIC. The Natya Stem Dance Kampni, which is the performing unit of the school, showcased Kathak's rich history through vintage and contemporary choreographies. With director Madhu Natraj as the sutradar and solo performer, the dance unit showcased impeccable kathak with tight and fast footwork interspersed with languid grace and expressions. Of all the classical dance forms, Kathak is arguably the most pan-Indian, given its popularity in both North and South India and its incorporation of the Ganga-Jamuna sanskriti (or Hindu-Muslim elements). Other classical dance forms are rooted in one state, whether it is Mohiniattam in Kerala or Bharatanatyam in Tamil Nadu.

Odissi is a dance form that I don't know very much, growing up as I did in Chennai. Nrityagram, which brought this dance form to Bangalore and South India, is alas too far away. Recently, I sat through a two-hour Odissi dance performance in ADA Rangamandira. Organized by dancer-teacher Madhulita Mohapatra, the annual festival titled Naman had three dance troupes perform. The first was Madhulita's own school, Nrityantar Academy of Performing Arts. This was followed by the Sutra Dance Theatre from Malaysia, founded by dancer-choreographer Ramli Ibrahim. The final act was by Devjani Sen's Odissi Dance Centre (ODC), based in Bangalore. All three performances showed me the physicality of Odissi in addition to its grace.

The most prestigious dance conference, the Natya Kala—held in December—is convened this year by

Bangalore's dancing couple Nirupama and Rajendra. One of the loveliest things that these founders of Abhinava Dance Company do is Madanotsav, a festival to welcome spring, conceived by Shatavadhani Dr R. Ganesh, a Bangalore-based Sanskrit scholar.

Of all the arts, I am drawn most to dance. And among dance, the one that I know best is Bharatanatyam. For this, I go to Praveen Kumar, a Bangalore-based Bharatanatyam dancer and guru who has trained legions of students. When my mother turned 80 a few years ago, she wanted a Bharatanatyam performance at her celebration. I turned to Praveen who had one of his students, Divya Hoskere (her mother, Anupama, does amazing things with traditional puppets, among other things), perform. Watching my mother's delight in this dance form was perhaps the best part of the celebration.

Ghibli art, AI and summer music concerts in the Garden City

The Bengaluru police has launched a series of social media posts in the format of Studio Ghibli, the viral art trend. This has artists protesting about how ChatGPT comes after not just our work but also our art. It seems unfair to see a process that was painstakingly perfected over decades, by Japan's Studio Ghibli, now being reproduced in seconds by AI. One the other hand, it democratizes art in a way that seemed out of reach for those who couldn't draw. All of which got me thinking about the arts and how they were going to be transformed by AI. Films are a given. Today, I saw an AI-generated film on Instagram about scuba divers exploring the Rama Sethu or the stone-bridge at the ocean floor, perfectly timed for the Sri Rama Navami festival that happens on April 6.

A friend wrote from America recently saying that they had been invited to a Sri Rama Navami function at a New Jersey temple. All of which is fine, except this friend is an observant Jew. He wanted to know what this festival was about. As an answer, I sent him a recipe for panagam, one of my favourite drinks. What makes this cooling drink special is the addition of dried ginger, which, in my opinion, provides the kick to the jaggery, lemon juice and cardamom powder combination that are the backbone of the drink.

This is the start of the Hindu festival calendar, a season of new beginnings. In my building, Maharashtrians celebrated Gudi Padwa last week, with a stick or Gudi with an upturned matka-type vessel on top to welcome the victorious Lord Rama. Telugu people sent us bevu-bella or neem-jaggery to celebrate the dawn of their new year: Ugadi or Yuga-aadhi. Our Muslim neighbours sent over sweets to celebrate Eid and the end of the holy month of Ramadan. So I have been feasting on Shrikhand, jaggery and halwa.

The other marker of this season was the 87th annual Ramaseva Mandali concert series. It started on 6 April 2025 with a Carnatic music concert by Sandeep Narayan, and ended on 2 May with a harikatha by Vishaka Hari. In between, several big names in Carnatic and Hindustani music performed at the Fort Auditorium in Chamarajpet. I have attended these concerts for many years and love them. They are held outdoors. The whole setup is modest and inclusive. The music is great. I met Karnataka politician Krishna Byre Gowda there over a decade ago. The only problem for me is the travel time from Ulsoor where I live to Chamarajpet, a leafy tree-lined area that I love. It takes over an hour. As a result, I pick and choose the concerts that I want to attend and stick closer to home otherwise. One of the places near my home that I visit is Urban Solace.

Urban Solace is a small café and performing spot that is walking distance to Ulsoor Lake. When it first opened years ago, residents on the tiny street complained about an increase in traffic and parking problems. Today, it has settled down to being a neighbourhood bistro. You can go in for their stand-up comedy which happens on Wednesdays, or to listen to poetry during their long-running Tuesdays with the Bard series. I began writing poetry after my father passed away in 2020. I believe it was his parting gift to me because he loved English poetry and used to recite it from memory. Today, after about 201 rejections (I counted), I have 20 poems published in journals. One has even won an award. So finally, and a little hesitantly, I have started calling myself a poet.

Last Tuesday, I went to Urban Solace to listen to poetry and also read two of my poems. It was an exhilarating experience. There is a small but tight community of poets in Bangalore, anchored by two worthy institutions: Atta Galatta, which holds poetry evenings, and Urban Solace. There is the online Non-Aligned Poetry Collective that puts together many performance poetry sessions as well. I have just dipped my toe into this world. Let's see what happens.

Indian poetry in English is one thing, but poetry in our own languages has a beauty that is unmatched. When I listen to Kannada, Tamil, Hindi or Urdu poetry, the words have a cadence that suits our tongue and how we speak. Sanskrit poetry too is the motherlode of the metaphors that populate our country. Years ago, when I conducted a Sanskrit podcast, poet Mani Rao told me that Sanskrit poetry often compared the flight of a flock of birds to the garland that hangs at the entrance of our homes. The way I access the beauty of Sanskrit is through an online group called the Bharatiya Vidvat Parishad (BVP) where everything from metaphors to music to metre of verses is discussed. Sure, there is politics as well, but if you ignore that, you get gems in poetry.

I tried to get ChatGPT to write a poem. It was adequate but too cohesive, too much like a well-thought-out argument. It didn't have the fractures of mind that make for great poetry. So, there you have it. Art can perhaps be replicated by AI, but the human ability to compose poetry cannot. At least not yet.

Subcultures and Identity

Rainbow on Church Street: Are straight people afraid of gay folks?

Recently, I was at the 14th edition of the Bengaluru Queer Film Festival (BQFF), a three-day community-funded event where 50 films were screened. The event took place at Medai, a performing arts space that, happily, has become part of the performing arts renaissance in Bangalore, where intimate spaces showcase interesting programmes. The films at BQFF reframed the narrative and gave 'voice to the unheard', according to the well-produced brochure handed out to visitors. I arrived on Day One, halfway through a Punjabi film. Following that was a Kannada feature film, *Dvamdva* (Duality), about a young yakshagana performer, Chukki, who plays female characters and says that he feels like a 'female trapped in a male body'. Directed by Kling Johnson, I found the film nuanced and layered. Set in Udupi, the film shows that queerness exists (and perhaps has always existed) in the broader swathe of society all over India with distinct vernacular names.

My friend who comes from Sakleshpura says that while queer folks are nowadays called 'gay' in Kannada, they used to be called 'Shikandi'. In Tamil, there are different names depending on who 'lies on top or the bottom' during the sexual act, according to queer folks I interviewed in Shivaji Nagar. You would think that a society like ours, used to such variations that existed, arguably from the time of the Puranas (where Shikandi was immortalized), would be just fine with diverse sexual orientations. The films at BQFF showed that this is both true and false.

Sure, there is a feeling, at least in cities like Bengaluru, that being queer is accepted these days by families and societies, partly because queer-ness has become part of collective conversation, and partly because many of us know folks who are gay. What I understood from the films I watched is that straight folks fear queer-ness for a couple of reasons. In *Dvamdva*, the parents of the title character love their son but are worried about societal ridicule. The other reason is that parents worry that their gay children will have 'loose' unhappy relationships. 'Being married to a normal person is hard enough,' is a frequently heard heteronormative comment. How to change this? My own trajectory is perhaps an example of this process.

Growing up in a conservative family in Chennai in the 80s, I had no idea about queer-ness till I went to a women's college, Mount Holyoke in Massachusetts, as a undergraduate. There, I encountered lesbians who educated me. Said my dorm-mate, Debbie, who shared the common showers down the hall: 'What are you afraid of? That I will jump you in the shower?' Actually I was.

In art school, my closest friend, Jennifer, happened to be gay and I learned about her life and love first-hand. We still remain friends. As a journalist in New York, my editor, Ted, was gay and in a relationship for decades. I visited his stylish spotless home in Brooklyn and knew his adopted son, now in college. Today, I know friends of my children who happen to be gay and are thriving. The point is that my route to overcoming my bias was through friendships. For me, the best way to understand and accept variations of any kind is by becoming part (at least peripherally) of that community. I am still learning. My kids constantly correct me for my incorrect heteronormative statements, and in fact, while writing this article, one of my fears is that I will say something that is not 'correct' and will come across as close-minded. The acid-test, at least in my mind in terms of realizing whether you truly accept variations, is the question: What if your child... And then fill in the blanks according to your bias. What if your child is queer? What if your child marries a Muslim/Hindu/Christian (depending on your religion)? What if your child marries a foreigner?

As far as the first question is concerned, I would like to think that I would accept it if my children were gay, although one can never be sure till it happens. My path to acceptance came because I have seen queer folks succeed and thrive in relationships and careers. Many of the writers I admire, or the fashion designers I follow, are at the pinnacle of their fields and happen to be gay. Thanks to the two friends I mentioned, I also know that relationships are not 'harder' if you are gay, that relationships can last, that two queer folks can have a marriage that is no different than others'—in countries where they can marry.

Being human is a gloriously varied, joyous and painful experience. The fact that identity these days—gender or sexual—is fluid is something that should be celebrated, not feared. Inside each of us lies a male aspect and a female aspect— we are all *ardhanaris*. Embracing both our male and female selves expands our life and thinking.

In India, I have many acquaintances who happen to be gay but just a few queer folks who I can call my friends. I define friendship as those who have visited my home more than one time, and those who I am regularly in touch with. By that metric, at least in Bangalore, I have very few queer friends. I would like to change that, which is perhaps why I attended BQFF in the first place.

Buying happiness under ₹100 in Cubbon Park and Jayanagar

There was a huge starfruit tree in the middle of Cubbon Park, the story goes. An old woman sat under the tree, gathered the fallen starfruit, cut them in half, sprinkled a mixture of salt and chilli powder on the cut fruit, and sold them to returning school children for a few paise. Everyone was happy: the old woman, the children, and the tree. Bangalore is full of apocryphal tales like this, ranging from the origin of its name. But this tale got me thinking about happiness and whether it was possible to access it for cheap—specifically for under ₹100. So here are some things that I have tried.

1. Every happiness study points to human connection as the real route to happiness. Aristotle said that humans are 'social' animals, which means that even if we call ourselves loners or introverts, connecting to humans will improve happiness. The new phrase for this is 'micro-moments of connection'. In India, we are blessed because we are surrounded by humans,

even at home. So the next time your milk-man, courier, postman, iron-man or flower-delivery rings your doorbell, think of connecting with them. You will be surprised at what ensues.

2. When a courier knocks on your door this winter season, take the package and say, 'Put on a sweater, why don't you? Bangalore is cold these days.' I guarantee you that it will put a smile on his lips and warm your cockles. If you can say this in Kannada, even better. You will experience a micro-moment of connection and joy.
3. To feel grateful is to feel happy. There are formal ways of doing this including keeping a gratitude journal and writing three things that you are grateful for. I have tried this but it didn't work for me—felt too forced and fake. These days, when I feel glad for my lot in life, I take a moment and savour it. The other day, I was walking through a tiny street in my neighbourhood. With its monkey-top roofs and blue doors, it felt like I was in Morocco or Greece. How lucky I am to live here and be able to walk around in great weather, I thought to myself.
4. Hug someone for more than 30 seconds. According to research, it takes about 30 seconds for the oxytocin to release while you are hugging.
5. Talk to kids. I learned this from my mother-in-law. She is 91 years old and walks around our building. Her face lights up when she sees kids. She makes it a point to say 'hello' to them and quiz them about their day. The kids also respond. They run towards her, hug her and tell her news. 'I got a new laptop

today, just for myself,' said one kid beaming. She was happy and so was my mother-in-law.

6. Speak to the staff who work in your office or building. I learned this from my mother. She is 86 and knows the name of all the housekeepers who clean our building. She knows the names of their children, the details of their lives, and what they need ('Do you have a spare sweater for Nandini,' Ma will ask).
7. Take a hike. Bangalore is blessed with many trails, all under two hours away. Take a hike on weekends to clear your head.
8. Bangalore is home to many arts organizations with free concerts and lectures. The Bangalore International Centre for one, also Atta Galatta, and then Gayana Samaja in Basavanagudi for free music.
9. Now we come to the paid part. Walk on Broadway Road off Shivaji Nagar and you will find old bakeries making bread, puff, naan and biscuits in the old-style brick 'bhatti" ovens. During Ramadan or Eid, the most sinful khoya (called khava in these parts) naans and sheermals are available. Buy one for ₹75, hot from the oven.
10. Tiny Kentacky (yes, that's the spelling) Chicken Corner on Richmond Road serves hot idlis and dosas brought out to your car for ₹70. Dosa with chicken curry costs more.
11. While it's quite commercial, Chalukya Samrat, now in Sobha Mall near Church Street, has been serving terrific badam halwa, dosas and idlis since 1977. Try their rawa idli with ghee for ₹95.
12. Have a by-two coffee (allows one to divide one cup

by two people) in any darshini. It will ensure that you are going with someone, which in the end is the point of the whole thing.

Happiness is subjective, hard to measure and fleeting. A Christian Dior bag can make one person happy, while another may get turned on by a rare video-game. Objects can only take you so far though, and I say this as a person who loves objects. Yearning for an object, saving up for it, and waiting to buy it is almost as pleasurable (or perhaps more joyous) than actually getting it. So the next time you want to give someone a Christmas or New Year's gift, give them something that they can savour for weeks. Tell them what you are giving them, and tell them that it will come in a few weeks. They will enjoy the wait as much as the gift. Better yet, give them the gift of your company. Take them out for a movie, a meal, a dancing, a hike, or just shopping. They will be happy, and guess what, you will be too.

Secret Bangalore: 25 things to try

Republic Day is coming up and preparations at every stadium in Bangalore are in full swing. The Indian Republic is so gloriously varied and vibrant, which got me thinking about my own city. Today, Bangalore is known for its startups, IT companies and billionaires. However, there is another Bangalore, hiding in plain sight between the Porsches and power couples. Here below is a list of 'Secret Bangalore' suggestions, in honour of India's 75th Republic Day.

1. Drink coconut water from the seller adjacent to the Conrad Hotel. This physically challenged coconut seller has been at the site for decades.
2. Have a kachori at Sudha Chaats on Berlie Street. Run by a mother-and-son, and open in the early evening, this humble eatery serves bajjis, kachoris or samosas to a loyal customer base. Also try Gullu's chaats on Serpentine Road, Tikki Adda in Jayanagar, Bangarpet chaats in Domlur, Naidu chaats in Basaveshwara Nagar, Gangotree in Chalukya Circle, Kedias Fun Food in Jayanagar (try the rasgulla chaat here), and Sri Sairam

Chaats and Juice in Malleshwaram. The flavours are all slightly different but all promise hygiene and taste.

3. Fresh juices are a very Bangalore thing. Try the juices in edible carved fruit bowls at Eat Raja outlets in Jayanagar, Malleshwaram and TC Palya, all promising 'zero-waste' juice.
4. Go to Sri Raghavendra Stores in Malleshwaram for idli, vada and chutney (no sambar), and shavige (vermicelli) bhaath.
5. Visit Accurate Demolisher and Furniture in St. John's Church Road opposite Coles Park. Like many antique shops, wander inside for an Alice-in-Wonderland experience—from chairs to Chinese vases, lacquer trays to fake apple trees. Talk to the owner, Iqbal, for tales of old Bangalore.
6. Koramangala is known for its giant micro-breweries and roads lined with coffee roasters. But right near Koramangala police station is a lane lined with stalls serving hearty homely food, including momos.
7. Go to Desi Trust, a store near South End Circle. Founded by distinguished theatre people who care for handloom and craft, such as M.S. Sathyu, Prasanna, and Jayanthi Marulasiddappa, among others, this is a great store to visit for authentic handloom products.
8. Stationery stores abound all over Bangalore, but visit the roads parallel to Ibrahim Sahib Street for Italian paper that you can get custom-cut to fit your Hermes diary as I have done. Thick paper, bespoke size, what's not to like.
9. Bangalore has a large community of fountain-pen lovers. Nitin Pai, co-founder of Takshashila Institution,

told me about Rathnam Pens, used by Mahatma Gandhi. I ordered one. Unfortunately it leaked. But I buy fountain-pen inks of various colours at RBK Pens near Church Street.

10. V.S. & Sons bookstore is to Basavanagudi what Book Worm and Blossoms bookstores are to Church Street.
11. Any store with the word 'Condiments' in its name ought to be visited. You never know what you will get there, but they will likely be authentic Kannadiga delicacies. Try Manjunatha Condiments in DVG Road and Srinivasa Condiments (Subbamma Stores) near Gandhi Bazaar.
12. To live in Bangalore and not eat a bajji singles you out as an immigrant. Try Vinayaka Bajji in NR Colony, Basavanagudi, for Kundapura-style capsicum or onion bajji. Try Annapoorneshwari Bajji Centre in Jayanagar.
13. South Bangaloreans have an affection for Kundapura as a haven for great food. Anywhere you find Kundapura masala, buy it. Anywhere you find jackfruit-leaf kadubu, buy it. Anywhere you find Coorg coffee, buy it.
14. Siddoji & Sons has been selling clothes in DVG Road, Basavanagudi, since 1925. It is where you go if you want to buy 20 well-priced sarees of good quality. The same applies to Girija Silks in Malleshwaram.
15. SN Refreshments or Shankara Narayana Refreshments in JP Nagar is like many beloved darshinis of Bangalore—the place to go for hot idlis, vadas, kesaribhath and dosa. There are others like this all over Bangalore—Veena Stores in Malleshwaram, Brahmins in Chamarajpet, and Adigas in Ulsoor.

16. If Japanese food is your favourite, go to Azuki, widely favoured as Bangalore's best Japanese.
17. Windmills Craftworks in Whitefield is the original stomping ground for mixing music and beer. Check out the listings and definitely go if there is jazz on.
18. If you are a gadget nerd, go to the Samsung Experience Centre at the Bangalore Opera House for sleek gadgets in a historical setting.
19. The Bangalore International Centre and Rangashankara are at different sides of the city but always have something going on.
20. Hatworks Boulevard is an oasis on Cunningham Road. There are designer stores, restaurants and, best of all, green spaces.
21. Indiranagar is full of restaurants. Consider a coffee crawl beginning with Humble Bean—try the cold brew tasting flight.
22. Nandi Hills is a cliché but go with a group for the Skandagiri sunrise trek.
23. Organized by Pachaak, the New India Lodge 1950s is an immersive theatre and food experience. Visit the Instagram page of Urbanauts to find out details of current and upcoming shows.
24. The Rezwan Razak Museum of Indian Paper Money is a place I have been wanting to go to.
25. Hug the fig tree in Cubbon Park or the giant silk cotton tree in Lalbagh.

From Basavanagudi to UB City: Two Bangalores: Street and luxury

Anyone who says Bangalore is an expensive city has not been to Shivaji Nagar in the evenings. Forget the main Commercial Street. Take any of the small gullies to its right and walk down a few yards to Ibrahim Sahib Street, Veera Pillai Street and Lubbay Masjid Street. Here at street corners, you will find a plethora of modest restaurants serving tasty inexpensive food. Some have no names. It is just a lady sitting inside a storefront serving freshly made pakoras, dosas or boiled corn with toppings. One evening, I walked down Jewellers Street to U.P. Bhavan where an elderly husband and wife manned the counter (and, it seemed, the cooking). The wife was slicing and spicing green chillies that were served along with my ₹20 samosa order, topped with a sweet tamarind and green coriander chutney. As I stood awkwardly in the small space and tried to eat, the woman wordlessly moved the spices she had been mixing and asked me to sit and eat. 'Aaram se,' she said softly. Relax, enjoy the food. This was old-fashioned Indian hospitality.

The same with 4th Block market. You go there to shop for costume jewellery, puja items, or readymade kurtas. But you end up eating—a lot. Every street corner has push carts selling raw mango, cut watermelon, pani puri and spicy potato chips on a stick. You can easily spend a couple of hours here—people watching, shopping, and ducking into the tiny shops where you can find tailors who will repair your torn jeans, jewellers who will melt your gold jewels, and shopkeepers who will make fresh pillows stuffed with polyester fabric or (more expensive) cotton stuffing.

There are two Bangalores I inhabit and I love both. One is the world of fine dining, wine and luxury, and the other is the gullies and streets. I enjoy the 'luxury' Bangalore but I am head over heels in love with 'street' Bangalore. Rarely do these two worlds collide, but recently they did. I signed up for a mushroom foraging walk in Cubbon Park. We were about 15 people and followed an exuberant mycologist (someone who studies fungi, yeasts and mushrooms) named Hari for two hours hunting for mushrooms. They were everywhere. The next time you see dead trees or leaf litter, look around. You will see mushroom of all kinds around it. The walk was under the auspices of Nuvedo, founded by Jashin Hameed and Prithvi Kini (a husband-and-wife team). I came away with three bottles of mushroom extracts. They cost ₹1,500 per bottle, so they are not cheap, but they are good for health and help with sleep and digestion.

I took a couple of thimbles of cordyceps mushrooms on the day I went to Loya at the Taj West End for lunch.

The West End is a property like no other. When I visit, I touch the rain tree and look for woodpeckers near the back where a temple sits. Loya takes the place of Masala Klub and, frankly, I find the food and drink in this new avatar a lot better. This is slow cooking inspired by the Bakarwal shepherds of Jammu and Kashmir. The result is unusual dishes, smoked flavours, Indian-inspired cocktails, and generous use of expensive ingredients—*gucchhi* or morels for instance. I like dense, heavy food— paneer, dal makhani, chole—and my husband likes light food. Loya's food would satisfy us both.

What Bangalore lacks are regional flavours. Mangalore's food, for example, is underrepresented, even though there are countless 'Mangy Bangies', or Mangalorean Bangaloreans. Ouzo by Fire attempts to rectify this. It is a new standalone restaurant that serves ManGo cuisine or Mangalorean Goan, which means that it will forever be compared to 'how my Mom used to make this dish'. Seafood is the star here and the cocktails use jamun and kokum for flavour. I loved the fresh 'poi' breads and creative dips. Chef Milan Gupta is a fund of knowledge about coastal cuisine. I loved the sour taste of kokum that permeated many dishes, and the lightly spiced salads. Ghee roast—either the chicken or paneer version—is the star here and if you haven't tasted this, you really need to.

The Oberoi doesn't really do pop-ups but recently they did—to introduce their new chef,

Anirban Dasgupta. At his opening dinner, he created a menu based on his life story. He devised a menu where every dish was from the regions where he had cooked at—beginning with Bengal, then Goa, Jaipur, Delhi, the

Northeast and finally Bengaluru. With every dish, he had placed cards with his personal take on cuisine. This was a wonderful way to introduce a chef, a cuisine, and a story. The chef as storyteller, and along the way, showing off his prowess.

Where I end up after a night is at home with a book and a bottle of ginger kombucha. Bengaluru has a whole range of artisanal cheeses, kombuchas, breads and even paan. I keep trying many of them. As I write this, I am swigging a bottle of rose kombucha from Mossant Fermentary. It has been around for a while, but I like its new floral flavours—hibiscus, rose, and of course my go-to, ginger.

How do you end your day?

∞

South Bangalore marriages, ambition, and cheese: A motley guide

Politician Tejaswi Surya married Carnatic singer Sivasri Skandaprasad earlier this month with great fanfare and predictably some controversy. The BJP MP does not shy away from social media. He speaks his mind and does crazy things like opening an aircraft emergency exit. He doesn't seem to court controversy but doesn't shy away from it either. When he said not to bring bouquets, the florists took umbrage. In a video that he posted on X, he talks earnestly in Kannada about people waiting for hours to attend his wedding reception to bless him and his new wife. Surya is ambitious and wears his RSS opinions on his sleeve. He seeks attention and makes good choices, the latest being his choice of wife. All of which led me to wonder about ambition and adaptation.

In order to achieve anything in life, you need a few things: ambition, effort, persistence and luck come to mind. But one quality that is equally important is not spoken about as much. Ambition requires nimbleness and adaptation. You need to change your stance, quite literally sometimes.

Consider Bharatanatyam dancer Malavika Sarukkai, who premiered 'Beeja: earth seed' at Chowdiah Hall in Bengaluru. The bravura performance, supported by Rohini Nilekani Philanthropies, connected the flora and fauna of planet earth with story, song and dance. Lots of senior Bharatanatyam dancers including Praveen Kumar, founder of Chithkala School in South Bangalore, were in attendance. All spoke about how 'Mala-akka', as she is called, adapts and evolves the dance form that is her metier to suit the circumstance and time.

Dance, like sport, is physically demanding. Most sportspeople retire and become commentators or coaches to propagate their art. In the performing arts too, there are dancers who become equally renowned teachers, training legions of students in their gurukuls. Malavika takes a different approach. Through her trust, she endows and supports other dancers. But more than anything, she is a dancer. She has adapted the art to suit her body, age, and cultural zeitgeist that values themes of sustainability. Beeja is not traditional in its content and approach. Yet, at the same time, it is resolutely grounded in the Bharatanatyam *paddhati* or tradition.

It is not just individuals or artistes who need to do this. The best hotels of Bangalore continuously adapt their menus, approach and events to stay one step ahead of the game. The big hotel brands—the Oberoi, Taj, Leela, JW Marriott, Conrad and others—are equally adept at dancing in various ways to whet the appetites of their customers. They do pop-ups with visiting Michelin-starred chefs and change their approach to ingredients and execution. This involves imagination.

One of the cutest names that I've come across in recent memory is Kempe Gouda cheese from Melchior. I heard about this cheese brand from Anirban Dasgupta, executive chef of the Oberoi Bengaluru. Since his arrival at the hotel, Chef Dasgupta has championed local artisanal brands including with cheese. This is not common. The best hotels have access to global ingredients that are of consistent quality and therefore risk-free. To opt for local Indian brands like Eleftheria, Melchior and other cheeses may come at a lower price but also means more work for the kitchen to ensure consistent quality. The good thing is that such Indian artisanal products, whether it is Under the Mango Tree honey or local cheeses like Vallambrosa and Begum Victoria, lend themselves to storytelling.

Now that she is married to a popular politician, Sivasri Skandaprasad also needs to think about excellence and adaptation. For lovers of music and dance like me, Sivasri is a rock star—a bigger one than her husband. Her explanation of esoteric Oothukadu Venkata Kavi's compositions helped me when I learned one recently (Sadananda Mayi). She is already famous in music circles but now she traverses the challenging and occasionally dirty field of politics as well. How will she change? How will she adapt and yet retain the essence of who she is? One thing seems sure from her past career: she colours inside the lines, by which I mean that she follows the rules and stays true to tradition. To adapt, she may have to lose this earnestness that marks her public persona, and opt for some level of risk and playfulness. The best way to achieve that is through creative collaborations.

Bangalore in particular seems to encourage this ecosystem of collaboration as Vinay Varanasi has proved with his wildly popular MadRasana. He collaborates and combines his storytelling with different musicians, including Sivasri. The lightness of touch Varanasi brings to storytelling lends itself to the mood of the moment. He adapts tone and text to circumstance.

Adapt or die, says the quote, itself an adaptation of the original by H.G. Wells. The same could be said about gifted artistes, be they chefs, cheesemakers, singers, storytellers or dancers.

Durga on a BMTC bus: Goddess energy in the city

I have been watching *Aachar & Co* on repeat. This visually gorgeous film—with its limited colour palette, slow-motion movements, and period sets, all creating a self-contained universe set in Jayanagar in the 60s—reminds me of Wes Anderson's movies. The fact that the producer, director and composer are all women is irrelevant to the sensitive plot and spot-on dialogues in the film. With its Ambassador cars, ceramic *bharani* jars for mango pickles, traffic-free streets, and cotton-silk sarees, the film evokes nostalgia for the Bangalore of yore. Sindhu Srinivasa Murthy, the film's director who also plays the lead actress, is hugely talented. The ensemble cast bring to mind *The Royal Tenenbaums,* an Anderson movie, but here, the director's touch is lighter and defter. Composer Bindhumalini's eminently hummable songs and her riff on M.S. Subbulakshmi's famous suprabhatam are sure to put a smile on your lips if you happen to be South Indian and woke up listening to M.S.'s version every day of your childhood. Produced by Ashwini Puneeth Rajkumar, the film is a must-watch.

Part of the reason I loved the film is that it is female-centric without being soppy. South Indian movies, specifically Tamil and Kannada movies, treat women terribly. Women are cast as unidimensional characters sans strong emotions. Rajinikanth movies are the worst offenders in my view. Kannada films too are equally bad. *Mungaru Male,* the blockbuster hit, normalizes a guy who stalks a girl. In the film *Mr. & Mrs. Ramachari,* there is a stupid dialogue linking male-female relationships to cell phones, and crudely blaming the woman no matter what the situation.

Aachar & Co is a breath of fresh air. Here too, women play to stereotype (all the girls want to get married, which is perhaps true of that age), but they aren't opaque lacklustre heroines created only to please men. You see their complex inner lives, their petty jealousies, their grit amidst tragedy, and finally their redemption.

It seems especially right to highlight the movie now because you see, goddess energy is here—in the city and in the country. For nine nights, it is believed that Goddess Durga descends from the heavens and conquers evil. In terms of religion, I am riddled with internal conflicts. I am a Hindu but suspicious of its Godmen-seers. I love the rituals linked to all ancient faiths, but dislike the patriarchy inherent in them. Some of the greatest works of art—the Sistine Chapel, Sanskrit verse and Sufi music—are a result of faith. But I also see the petty hypocrisies inherent in all believers, all of which I wrote about in my previous book, *Food and Faith.* So too with Navarathri. It is a time when Indian patriarchy worships a goddess—she who rides a tiger and kills a buffalo-headed demon named Mahisha. For nine days and nights, women don silks and go visit each other's 'golu' dolls, sing and dance.

Female energy is different. Often the word used to describe it is 'softer', but this is not an accurate description. Goddess Durga is not the epitome of soft grace. She isn't any of those words that Indian girls are raised to live by—demure, soft, graceful, adjusting, or accepting. We see all these qualities in the women of *Aachar & Co*, but thankfully with a twist. Goddess Durga though doesn't play nice. She is aggressive, fearless and unflinching, qualities that you see in the women riding Bangalore's BMTC buses these days.

In a masterstroke, the Karnataka government has launched a Shakti scheme which allows women to travel free of cost on BMTC buses. Much has been written about this, about the freedom that it gives women, about groups of women with packed bags and snacks going from town to town. Two viral images include a female monkey travelling on a bus, and an old lady who bends and touches her forehead on the steps of the bus as she climbs in, saying that for the first time she can travel without asking for money from her children.

Years ago, Sheryl Sandburg posted a question: what would you do if you were not afraid? These women are quietly answering the question. For the first time, unafraid and unaccompanied, they are travelling in groups and by themselves to tourist spots, temples, picnics, and to visit friends and family. This is what women do when they are not afraid.

Perhaps because I take my own mobility for granted,

I had not realized how oppressed women are by their enforced immobility. In economically disadvantaged homes, women stay home mostly because they don't have the means or money to travel. This scheme changes both. They may still need permission to step out, but at least now they don't need to beg for money to travel.

NGOs such as Bangalore Moving and Alli Serona are trying to enable even more female movement by focusing on last-mile connectivity and more bus stops for women.

If our streets are safe for women to walk on, if our public transport—metros and buses—remain packed with women, then female energy will truly descend from the heavens, take over the city, and, dare I say, conquer evil.

Inclusive hospitality: Shefs at The Leela Bengaluru

Last week, my friend, the kathak dancer-choreographer Madhu Natraj, called with some news. 'You know, it is good that Mr Virendar Razdan is back in Bangalore because the arts and hospitality are once again getting connected,' she said.

Razdan is currently the general manager of the Leela Bharatiya City and what Madhu was talking about was an event that the hotel was putting together. Called 'Shefs of the Leela', it showcased some high-quality women chefs over a sit-down dinner.

The best part from a performing arts point of view was that the brand had contacted—and contracted with—the Natya Stem Dance Kampni, where Madhu is director, to perform that evening.

There are two industries that have been deeply affected by Covid: hospitality and the performing arts. It seemed fitting that the two were coming together in synergy. Madhu was inviting me to watch the show.

The evening was a revelation. Four talented women

chefs, Romy Gill, Sanjana Patel, Meha Kumar and Vanshika Bhatia, planned and executed a four-course dinner for about sixty Bangaloreans. The wait-staff was also largely women—young girls, actually. The event was conceived by two women, Rupali and Akanksha Dean, and executed by The Leela hotels. Captain Nair, the late founder who named the brand after his wife, would have been proud.

I love hotels. I love the hospitality business. I think India excels in this area because, like Thailand, hospitality is hardwired in our cultural DNA, notwithstanding the tired slogan that we often trot out: Athithi Devo Bhava.

But what about inclusion and diversity—something every brand today talks about. Talk is cheap though. What counts is putting your money where your mouth is.

In 2022, there was an interesting study done to examine female participation in the workplace. The organizations (their names are a mouthful, I warn you) commissioning the study were the Women's Indian Chamber of Commerce & Industry (WICCI) Hospitality and Tourism branch, the Indian School of Hospitality (ISH), and Brigade Hospitality. Launched by the Indian government's Ministry of Tourism, the study highlighted several trends.

The good news was that hospitality as a field lent itself to female participation, and indeed, globally more women work in this field than ever before. However, most of these women work in junior levels—front office, housekeeping, communication and some service. But each of these women in the hotel business faced barriers unique to the field, according to Dr Payal Kumar, the lead researcher.

Within departments, women were pigeon-holed by bosses and colleagues into certain roles that were deemed 'safe' and 'not heavy' in both the literal and figurative sense. They were treated paternalistically by their bosses. I have seen chefs address junior female employees as *beti* or 'young lady'. They may mean well, but young women don't have to be betis. They can be 'badasses', which is a compliment by the way.

The hardest negotiations that women have to do are within their own homes. On the individual level, women who aspired to rise in hospitality faced more work-life pressures than their male counterparts. They had to go home after a full shift and take care of elders, in-laws and children. This is not unique to hospitality though.

The second prejudice was the assumption that they couldn't work late nights because, well, they were women. Even this has been addressed by many hotels that provide late-night transportation to employees.

The last one is deeper and harder to change. Men were sent to networking events, road shows, conferences and sales meets because, well, it was assumed that women could not network well. They could not push the agenda of the hotel. They were not aggressive enough to close deals. What do you do with this kind of mindset, which is just patently wrong?

As Dr Payal said, 'The study makes it clear that for women in India to reach the top of the booming hospitality industry, they not only need talent and drive but also deep structures of organizational and familial support.'

In other words, give your female employees a chance, guys (and most hotel GMs are, more often than not, guys).

I think what the Leela is doing is good because it is showcasing women who have overcome these prejudices.

If someone asks me for a solution to inclusion, I have a one-line answer: hire, promote, pay and invest in more women. Because this will create a ripple effect beyond what you can imagine. Young women who are eager to enter the hospitality industry need role models.

That evening, four confident women chefs came up on stage and talked about their creations. The icing on the cake was having the Natya Stem Dance Kampni interpret and connect the rasa of food with the rasa of dance.

'Rasa' is an unexplainable Sanskrit word. You can only experience it—and that night, we did.

BBMP to RWAs: A Bangalore year in review

It is that time of year—the time for renewals, new beginnings and resolutions. With the last one, I am both an optimist and a pessimist. While in a funk, I ask myself why I make resolutions since I don't persist with them anyway. But come this time of year, I make resolutions anyhow.

I think a New Year's resolution is an expression of hope. It is built on the idea that this year, finally, we will tick off all those things that we have been yearning to conquer—lose weight, exercise, learn embroidery, recite Urdu *shairis* (sonnets), dance the samba. Some take the opposite approach. They don't make resolutions and make grand pronouncements like 'I don't make resolutions; I keep them.'

I make tons of resolutions. My success record is patchy. This year, I pulled up all my written resolutions over the years to create a survey of my New Year's resolutions—and also to unpack what was possible to follow through and what was not.

So here below are my resolutions through the years and my current comments in parenthesis. I hope they give you inspiration, if not hope. The resolutions are not in chronological order.

November 2019: Next year—2020—I will savour every meal in every restaurant as if it were my last meal on earth. (And then Covid struck and I couldn't eat out at all.)

December 2006: The year I moved to Bangalore: I will fight for a cleaner city, since this is the city I and my children are henceforth going to call our 'home'. (This actually worked. I got involved in my RWA [Residents Welfare Association], went and met my corporator, and tried to work with the Pourkarmikas or PKs, which is what the Bengaluru Bruhat Mahanagara Palike (BBMP) calls the women who sweep our roads.)

2011: This year, I will try to get to know myself better. I will be at peace, then spread that to others in my orbit. (What a fail! I spread mayhem all around and particularly in my family.)

2015: This year, I won't fight with my husband. Or rather, I will fight differently with my husband. I won't use the tried-and-tested phrases. 'You always...you never.' Or, 'Yes, you did that nice thing...but...' (This resolution worked, for just one fight, before I resorted to the old arsenal of our marital fighting methodologies. I blame emotion. When you are pissed off, it is hard to remember your resolution.)

2017: I resolve to begin drawing like I did when I was seven years old. In fact, I resolve to begin singing like I did when I was ten. (This worked. I still doodle and sing—not well but enough. I doodle during meetings and sing when I walk down the stairs—every staircase has fantastic acoustics.)

2020: I plan to get in the best shape of my life so I can beat my husband at marathon hikes. And while I am at it, I want to achieve world peace. (Both were fails but the latter was a bigger fail than the first.)

2009: 2009 is a great year for Bordeaux wines. Buy a lot of them. (Which I did. And I am drinking some now.)

2021: Three resolutions interconnected: for me, my world and the world. For me: relinquish the title of 'The Great Procrastinator', although I am inclined to think about that one for a while. For my world: stop fighting with my kids. For the world: include beauty in any human endeavour. (All three are ongoing.)

2022: I will lift weights. (So finally, I found a trainer in my own building which allowed the five-year-old resolution of fitness to find fruition. This is actually a happy-ending story. Contact me if you want her number. And realize that you need help if you want to achieve your fitness goals. Unless you are some crazy disciplined person who only drinks kombucha and runs ultra-marathons in your spare time.)

2008: Let's be positive this year. New Year's resolutions are fun, even if I fail at them in a month. This year, I will make a simple resolution. I will learn a new language. And I will enjoy my children because guess what, soon they will become adults and be gone from my home and into the world. (This too was a successful year, because I learned Kannada. As for enjoying my kids, I really only did that after they left home, so be easy on yourself—all you young moms.)

Conclusion: Lots of podcasts tell us that the key to successful New Year's resolutions is to keep them simple. In other words, don't resolve to change your diet when you don't have time to drink even a single protein shake. Breaking down your resolutions into small parts will help. The best resolutions are usually borne of desperation. Think of all those nerds whose resolution year after year is to 'get laid', or those nature-loving desperados whose resolution is to see a black panther in Kabini within the year. Out of desperation comes resolution and out of that comes action. So don't give up hope, bro. Just keep at it.

What's your New Year's resolution? As for mine, it is to renew my relationship with yoga.

Sankranti and science in Sankey Tankey: Science, song, and sun

On 13 January, I attended two events on the same day: one supporting science and the other supporting underprivileged students.

The Infosys Science Prize is one of the most prestigious awards in India. Of the six laureates for 2023, two were women, a formula that the Infosys Science Foundation has followed for the last three years. Since its inception in 2008, a majority of the awardees are men. Only in 2017 was it balanced in terms of gender: 3 men and 3 women got the prize. In 2015, 2012 and 2011, all the awardees were male. I am waiting for the year in which the roles are reversed and a majority of women get the Prize and nobody even remarks about it.

The paucity of women in positions of power and prestige in science is a complex topic, with no straightforward takeaways or solutions. While more women are entering the sciences, they are a rarity in the top echelons of the field—much like in most other sectors. Leadership roles including those in juries are largely held by men.

It is tempting to make the 'old boys club' argument as a reason why women get short shrift in the sciences. With the Infosys prize, I am sure the male-dominated jury will make the case that their choice of awardees is based on merit and not gender. But as a woman, I know that finding women to nominate for panels, talks and awards is harder—men spring to the top of all of our minds. Unless juries make an effort, finding worthy women is always harder but that doesn't mean that exceptional women don't exist. Correcting for implicit biases and a higher search cost is an essential first step. For that to happen, perhaps the male domination in the composition of award juries needs to change.

From the Infosys Prize ceremony, I went to attend an Indian Ocean concert where all the proceeds went towards helping an NGO called Enabling Leadership that does terrific work with underprivileged children. It always surprises me how many worthy NGOs exist in India. I had not heard of Enabling Leadership but like their approach. Rather than concentrate on curriculum, they enable leadership through sport, art and play. It was great to watch young girls talk about playing football as a path to becoming a leader.

As a band, Indian Ocean are true originals. They did Indian folk-rock music before anyone else. They have a charming stage presence and played all their hits including the pleasing 'Kandisa'. The following day, Thaikkudam Bridge played to a sell-out crowd, also to benefit Enabling Leadership. Of the two bands, the music experience was better with Indian Ocean. Thaikkudam Bridge threw it all in and it was all too much. Drums drowned the vocals, strobe lights blinded the audience, and technicolour film clips continuously played as a distracting backdrop. I wish this energetic band would realise that they don't need all these pyrotechnics to capture the audience's attention. Their music is good enough. No matter. I felt that my ₹4,800 ticket was money well-spent, considering that it would benefit eager, ambitious young kids who are the future of India.

This week is the beginning of Uttarayan. We celebrated it here in Karnataka on 15 January as Makara Sankranti. I love our festivals. They are linked to season, earth and sky in ways that are profound and moving. Sankranti is among the most important because it signifies that the sun will move from Dhanu (Sagittarius) to Makara (Capricorn) in the Indian lunar calendar—which is different from the Gregorian Western calendar. Like most harvest festivals, Sankranti honours the sun. My mother does this by offering her morning coffee to the sun God before she drinks it. Today, I did the same. I did another thing that my mother always did during festivals. She used to take a walk to the market to get into the 'mood' of the festival. Now, she is too old to take the long walk to my local Shivaji Nagar market, but I did it on my own. It was the best part of my day.

Sugarcane stalks were piled high on the street, alongside fresh young turmeric stalks, stacks of betel leaves, white pumpkins, hyacinth beans (called *mochai* in Tamil and *avarebele* in Kannada), sweet potato, fresh peanuts and flower garlands. Buyers and sellers bargained spiritedly and the communal spirit was energizing and entrancing. The most interesting thing I learned was that villagers tie five types of leaves together in the entrance of the house as a *kaapu* or talisman to protect the family. The five leaves are neem, mountain knotgrass (*Aerva lanata*—called *sirupeelai* or *ponga-poo* in Tamil), dark tulsi or holy basil (called *karunthulasi* in Tamil and *Ocimum sanctum* in Latin), Thumbai or *Leucas aspera* leaves, and Avaaram flowers (*Senna auriculata*). If you look them up, you will find that they all have medicinal properties and are used as a talisman to ward off evil. So I tied these and kept them at the centre of my home to purify and better my environs.

The sun is sacred to most old cultures and now this central figure in our solar system has begun his long march north—beginning a period of renewal, rejuvenation and auspiciousness, all symbolized by a new harvest. Happy Sankranti, folks.

Bangalore wellness: Can—and should—spas go beyond ayurveda?

Ultimately, it comes down to the smell of the towels, I said when a Bangalore visitor asked why I had not given a spa guide to the city in this column. After all, I had written about everything else. This is odd because you see, I am that cliché. I am a spa junkie.

There are two types of people: those who love spas like me, and those who don't, like my husband. The third category is those folks who will have a *maalish-wali* or masseuse come home. This article is not for them. They see the massage as a utility, something that fosters health, which it does. But for me, the spa is an experience that cocoons you. It is a splurge.

Bangalore has many standalone spas including Bodycraft, Meraki, GlamsJo, and SPA.ce. All of these will give you a perfectly serviceable massage for between ₹2,500 and ₹3,500. But if you want the luxury experience, you have to go to a five-star hotel and shell out around ₹7,000 for a 60-minute massage. That is my method. I don't do it often, but when I can, I prefer the splurge.

Over my 20 years of being in this city, I have tried pretty much every five-star hotel's spa in Bengaluru. I tend to choose a newer hotel, because the towels smell better—or rather, they don't smell at all. I have pretty much given up on 'Ayush-type' ayurveda places in the city because all the towels smell of oil. When in doubt, choose a newer hotel. That is my first tip.

Recently, I was at the Four Seasons Infuse spa. It was heavenly. The towels were fresh. It was on a weekday morning and I was the only one there. This, too, is a strategy. Business hotels tend to be empty during the weekday, so if you have flexibility—go at 10.30 a.m. on a Tuesday, not a Monday. The masseuses work hard on weekends and so they are tired on Monday. Tuesday morning is better. I had the 'Flower at Four Seasons' which uses aroma oils inspired by the gardens of this city. As always, I took full advantage of the steam shower and the sauna before and after the treatment. I left my phone in the locker during the course of the massage, which you should do.

For Indian spas, coming up with creative ways to stay rooted to place is tricky. We have ayurveda, but then the question becomes: should you stay true to ayurveda as the CGH Earth brand tries to do? Do you make it luxury ayurveda? The Taj group does this well with rituals that are authentic and, indeed, moving. Or do you go beyond ayurveda and choose new paradigms in the spa segment?

The Four Seasons did this by linking it to the city and its gardens. The Shine spa at the Sheraton Grand Whitefield pays homage to Bangalore through its products—using sandalwood wraps and coffee scrubs. Frankly, I went to Shine because it is rated number one in spa and wellness in Bangalore's Tripadvisor. It is a spa of choice for many of my friends in Whitefield but not for me because I live an hour away. But here's the thing: If you go to Whitefield from central Bangalore, there are two options: one is to rush in and out, the second is use the time to do things you've been wanting to do in that area. I chose the second option. I had a beer at Rogue Elephant round the corner, shopped a bit, and had the Shine's signature massage which includes a variety of their techniques, all of which induce deep sleep.

But mostly in Bangalore, people tend to stick to their own locations. I live in Central Bangalore and so I only go to spas in this region. For value for money, nothing beats The Lalit. It is an old-style luxury hotel with lots of space right next to the golf course. The Rejuve spa was my go-to before Covid. Even now, you can get a 60-minute massage for ₹3,750. I usually go for their *njavara kizhi*, which is a straightforward ayurveda treatment that depends on the quality of the rice and medicinal herbs that are tied up into a poultice and applied on the body. Luxury hotels have the wherewithal to order good ingredients. And so it is at the Lalit. If you care about ingredients in a massage—good-quality oils and herbs, then you need to choose spas that won't take shortcuts.

This then is my case for splurging on spas. There will be a flower floating on the ground when you look down from the massage table. The linen will be fresh and clean, and not smell of anything. The quality of the products will be good. They will afford you privacy, which is rare in Bangalore. And they will give you space and time to just luxuriate. I tend to choose spending on experiences over objects so it is easy for me to choose spa treatments. You may be the kind of person who believes that you can buy a dress for ₹7,000 rather than a massage, in which case this entire article will not apply to you.

When science misses the plot: Bangalore's storytelling problem

In a brilliant stroke, ISRO has announced that it will send Prime Minister Modi to space. This does what science is rarely able to do: link human interest to science. Will this change now that the PM has aligned himself with the field? What can we do about this?

A lot has been written about this topic. Interviews with top scientists usually elicit two issues with the way science is being handled in India. One is a 'patchy' ecosystem with small clusters of scientific institutions not talking to each other. The second is funding from the government, which either trickles down or out.

Science has a storytelling problem and it begins with how scientists are educated. They are trained well in their topics of research but have little or no humanities training, particularly in communication. I would argue that every Masters or Doctoral programme in science ought to have a module in journalism and communication, in science writing for the lay public, in articulation and rhetoric. Along with explaining their thesis to their advisors, perhaps scientists should have a session where they explain their research to their non-scientific peers. This will connect them to the world at large beyond the corridors of research.

One example of a group of scientists who have done this successfully can be found the field of ornithology. Today, there is a worldwide movement of birdwatchers that use products created by the Cornell Lab of Ornithology including an app to identify birds, and Instagram pages which allow birdwatchers to access live cameras placed near the nests of owls, raptors and seabirds. Many people begin as amateur birdwatchers and then go deeper into the field. Pretty soon they are taking ornithology courses, reading research papers on bird migrations and morphology of parakeet necks. It is a short step to connect with scientists who work at the National Centre for Biological Sciences (NCBS) and attend lectures on specific and esoteric ornithology subjects. NCBS is a specific example in which the lay public visits to access specific science. But should Bangalore's scientific institutions make themselves accessible to the general public?

This too is a tough question because each scientific institution is a vibrant community of students, faculty and staff that have enough to think about and have no time really to expand their boundaries. Sure, many of them do this with a visitor's day and public lectures. But the results of a consistent connection with the public at large can only be gauged after a few years of doing this. And this needs to be led from the top—by directors and senior administration officials. There needs to be an office of communication, some amount of PR, some coaching to help faculty speak in public forums, and a desire to engage with the general public. I believe such an outreach will have positive results for the institution in question in ways that cannot be predicted. But in the meantime, we need organizations that connects science to society. Science today operates in silos that the public cannot access.

Let me put it another way. I used to be part of the programming committee of the Bangalore International Centre (BIC). A group of us would get proposals for various events in order to vet if they were suitable for our general-interest audience. If you created a graph, the greatest number of proposals were from publishers and authors, then from performing artists, then from social scientists and public policy researchers. Science would fall in the lower quartile. We as a committee tried to change it. We reached out to scientific institutions to see if they might be interested in doing a panel discussion or have a scientist speak on a topic that would be of interest to a general-interest audience. It was difficult to do. Unlike the arts, science does not lend itself to mass consumption. Some of it is simply the complexity of the subject matter. Theoretical physics and nano technology cannot (and you could argue, should not) dilute its complexity to suit a lay audience. This is esoteric stuff, understandable to specialists. It is not for the rest of us. On the other hand, scientists have successfully connected with the general public in ways that are diverse and interesting. Even Einstein, whose theory of relativity is understandable to just a miniscule portion of scientists, made himself relevant to the larger audience by writing about metaphysical and philosophical questions, taking a stand on public issues, playing the violin, and being a character. So too with Richard Feynman, whose wit and humour are on display in his books. Ditto for Carl Sagan and Stephen Hawking, who unpacked their specialized fields in books for the lay public. Why can't Indian scientists do this as well?

Science needs to connect with the general public in ways that don't involve the prime minister of the country.

What Bengaluru's science institutions do wrong

Here is a fairly stunning statistic, to use the tempered language of science. In the 2023 *Nature* Index of the top science cities globally, only one Indian city made it to the top 100. Guess which one? Bengaluru. Beijing was number one in top scientific output. New York City was number two. Predictably, the list has a disproportionate number of American and Chinese cities. But given India's rising economic prominence, why are there so few Indian cities making inroads in science? And what can Bengaluru do to improve itself in the scientific arena?

Historically, scientific advances happen in two ways. One is the lone scientist, working in isolation and doing groundbreaking research that leads to new paradigms. Let us call this the solitary genius 'invention' approach. The second, more common way is through collaborations—both with people within the field and also through intersections outside their field. Let us call this the 'ecosystem' approach. Bengaluru as a city can contribute to the ecosystem approach more than the invention approach.

Although laypeople think of scientists as a hyperspecialized species who operate in silos, they are actually good at collaborations—even at the global level. The only problem is that scientists keep track of other scientists in their specialist area. Cross-pollination within scientific areas, let alone with the general public, is rare—not just in India but also globally. Bangalore has a chance to change that.

There are 41 listed scientific institutions in Bangalore. They include the Indian Institute of Science (IISc), National Centre for Biological Sciences (NCBS), National Institute of Mental Health and Neurosciences (NIMHANS), National Institute of Advanced Studies (NIAS), Ashoka Trust for Research in Ecology and the Environment (ATREE), Raman Research Institute, and Indian Institute of Astrophysics, to name just a few. No matter what the scientific field, it seems, there is an institute in Bangalore that studies it. The problem is that these institutes rarely intersect with the general public.

That may change with the opening of the new Science Gallery. Founding director Jahnavi Palkey is a historian of science and has a keen sense of how to bring science to the people. This requires unpacking science in language that more people will understand. It also involves creating an ecosystem where researchers can intersect with each other and a wider circle so that 'ideas have sex', to quote the title of a book. The rough approach involves ensuring that scientists intersect with non-scientists on a regular and consistent basis. IISc is doing that with a series of lectures that brings dancers, authors and activists into their campuses. But in order for conversations to happen, it cannot be a one-off thing. A broad subset of diverse people need to run into each other in the IISc campus on a regular basis so that conversations can continue. This is happening at the Bangalore International Centre because of the range of its programming—and also because the audience mills around the lobby before each event allowing for tea and conversation.

Let me give you a personal example of the twists and turns in which ideas can collide. Recently, I was looking for solutions for osteo arthritis. I consulted two orthopaedics who were not able to help with the pain. I began looking at alternative therapies including Biodynamic Cranio-Sacral Therapy (BCST), which was developed by an osteopath. I read a helpful book on this topic called 'Accessing the healing power of the vagus nerve', written by Stanley Rosenberg, who is based in Denmark. I went to his website to see if he (or his students) taught workshops in India. Turns out that he has a link with the Sri Sri Ayurveda Hospital, which has an osteopathy division. Not being a disciple of Sri Sri Ravishankar, I needed to test out the waters so I went to their spa in Jayanagar called Sri Sri Wellbeing Spa. I had an excellent shirodara, abhyanga and steam there, and bought a few of their Shankara ayurveda lotions, because I had seen them at the Four Seasons spa. I also bought a non-caffeinated 'coffee' that is common in Tamil Nadu—called 'chukku malli coffee', it's made with dried ginger, cardamom, pepper, cloves and spices. Last week, I invited the Science Gallery's Jahnavi Palkey home and served her this coffee. She loved it and wanted to buy it.

So I directed her to the Sri Sri Wellbeing spa. But who knows? If she goes there, and onwards to the osteopaths at the Sri Sri Ayurveda hospital, she may come up with unusual connections between science, spirituality and wellbeing. Ideas having sex, really.

The question for the head of Bangalore's science institutions is: how to engender this type of cross-pollination on a regular basis?

⁂

What do Bangalore's youth really care about?

Is activism dead in Bangalore? I thought about this as I waded through knee-deep water in South Bangalore. Once again, the rains are upon us, and once again, the city is waterlogged.

Netizens in other cities are gleeful. Bangalore gets half the rain of Mumbai, and has half the population, said one. Yet it suffers from *more* flooding than Mumbai, every time it rains. What will it take for this city to wake up and get BBMP to do its job?

Am I living in Varthur or Venice, asked dancer Ramaa Bharadwaj on Facebook. We need gondolas to wade through our streets.

Does Bangalore lack the time or inclination to protest and seek good governance? Is it because we are an IT and tech city that keeps workers so busy that it induces brain fog for everything else?

One citizen, though, has taken action. Dhivya Kiran, 43, from Richmond Town has served a 50-lakh legal notice to BBMP stating that he has suffered 'physical agony and emotional trauma', directly because of Bangalore's potholed and damaged roads. On 14 May, his advocate K.V. Laveen served a legal notice that lists physical and emotional pain directly caused by Bangalore's roads: jerky stop-and-go traffic resulting in 'severe neck and back pain', which had him make four emergency trips to the hospital and orthopaedic doctors. Well done, I say. Finally.

It is not as if Bangalore doesn't have citizens' groups. The list is long. There are organizations like Oorvani which publishes *Citizen Matters*, a great read for those who want to keep in touch with civic action groups and their activities. I Change Indiranagar, HSR Citizen Forum and other Residents' Welfare Associations (RWAs) have been mobilizing their neighbourhoods. National organizations like Janaagraha began in Bangalore. Some offer channels of intersection between government and society: Bangalore Political Action Group (BPAC), Rise up for Rights, and Friends of Lakes come to mind. In addition, groups like Namma Bengaluru Foundation, Aravani Art Project, CIVIC Bangalore, Flourishing Bengaluru Collective, and many others have taken initiatives to make governance accountable.

What is interesting though is that many of these efforts are spearheaded by land-owning, home-owning middle-aged folks. Remember when colleges were the hotbed of protests? Well, that doesn't seem to happen in Bangalore; which leads me to the question: what do Bangalore's youth care about? What uniquely animates Bangalore's youth relative to say Delhi, Mumbai, Shanghai or San Francisco?

Sure, all these cities have ambitious, insecure, anxious,

eco-conscious, evolved young people. Some even ditch their jobs to volunteer, write poetry, climb mountains, and start companies. The problem though is the immigrant nature of Bangalore's population. Attend any launch event in Central Bangalore, and you'll hear Hindi, not Kannada. Upwardly mobile Bangaloreans, it seems, are from elsewhere. They move to Bangalore attracted by its cosmopolitan populace, great weather and startup culture. Bangalore thus has become a city of immigrants, where nobody takes ownership of its issues (save a few patron saints of lost causes). Why would people protest when Bangalore seems better than where they came from?

The second reason for this lack of activism is what the city does to your psyche. At the end of the day, Bangaloreans—like many South Indians—are not inherently flashy. We keep it down-and-low. Our humble-bragging and hustling is restricted to LinkedIn. This is the problem. Where is the time to protest and join parades when you are happy eating benne dose in CTR or birdwatching in Cubbon Park? The simmering prolonged discontentment that needs to happen in order for collective action to take place simply doesn't exist here because the Bangalorean is inherently live-and-let-live in nature.

But back to the question: what do Bangalore's youth care about? If I had to pick one, I would say that they yearn for community, perhaps because they move here sans family or friends, to get a job, most often at a startup, where they are surrounded by rootless folks just like them. If you are in your 20s or 30s in Bangalore, you learn quickly to join groups, to speed-date, to attend art, yoga, journalling or hand-pan music workshops, to enrol in improv theatre classes, and go to niche clubs for board games, manga, anime and quiz. All that coding during the day must result in a longing for something physical and sexual because dance classes are huge, ranging from pole dancing to salsa to get this— lap dancing. It seems that finally, a city that was defined by tech is learning to embrace the humanities, and here lies my hope.

In order to save the world, you have to read Homer and enjoy Keats. You have to read U.R. Ananthamurthy and Kuvempu, attend Shivarama Karanth's yakshagana revivals, learn to draw like Hebbar, and attend performances under Chowdiah's violin. The humanities humanize us. They make us care. They allow for empathy. If you are sitting in a cubicle, you won't care about the woman wading through water. The great thing about the comeback of the arts into Bangalore's ecosystem is that it offers hope for a more empathetic society. Cross-pollination between the worlds of art and tech may nudge us to collectively demand better governance from our politicians and bureaucrats.

So yes, activism may have been dead in Bangalore during the go-go years of IT. But thanks to art, theatre and music, it may well make a comeback.

Everyday Life and Introspection

When your NRI relatives come for wedding shopping in Bangalore

It is a truth universally known that NRIs who need to shop for a wedding usually come to India. We each have our own list of products, shops and people. This one is mine. Bangalore folks: if your NRI relative asks for wedding shopping suggestions, just send them this article.

Disclosure: I have no conflict of interest in recommending the below vendors. I have used some of them and have disclosed this as such. This is not a comprehensive list by any means.

Wedding shopping for South Indians used to be mostly sarees, except these days most brides want lehengas and dresses. Raw Mango has a store here in a lovely old bungalow. It is worth visiting. Right across the street is Good Earth, where my kids buy bedspreads to take to college. For sarees, here are the shops I would recommend.

Vimor: I love going to Vimor because Pavithra Muddaya champions weavers and doesn't mess with traditional handwoven designs. I attended a Christian wedding recently, where the bride wore a stunning bespoke Vimor saree. If you want something like this, you need to email Pavithra in advance and give her time to get a bespoke saree done.

House of Angadi: This is another beloved Bangalore brand that made waves when Deepika Padukone wore a saree from them for her wedding. I take TamBrahm brides to their Jayanagar outlet for the traditional nine-yards. Currently run by Radharaman, who shows his label Alamelu at Printemps Paris, visit their newest House of Angadi for a dedicated trousseau section.

Vijayalakshmi Silks: Another hoary Bangalore brand with heavy silks of the kind I like. The only problem is that this brand too has moved into the floral and vine patterns borrowed from Benaras, perhaps to please the large North Indian population in Bangalore. Then again, Angadi does this too. If you want traditional old-fashioned Kanchipurams, you really have to search.

Prasiddhi, Nalli, Varamahalakshmi Silks, and Taneira are other shops where you can look for silk sarees. Disclosure: I did some content work for Taneira, and through this work, I know that they have a handloom network and big ambitions for becoming a pan-Indian presence much like their jewellery arm, Tanishq. This helps when you want to return or exchange sarees.

ffolio: This was Bangalore's first multi-brand fashion store. Yasho Shroff has a good eye for that balance between timeless and trendy. She stocks subtle and lovely sangeet and mehendi clothes—for both men and women. Crafted yet practical, the designers she stocks have wide appeal and will work both for Indian weddings and cocktail wear.

Commercial Street is a must-visit for wedding shopping,

as is Jayanagar 4th Block. I don't know Jayanagar as well, so my recommendations are all from 'Comm Street', which I visit often. Liberty Silks is a good place to start if you want relatively inexpensive lehengas. Mysore Saree Udyog used to be a small store but now has floors of fabric that Bangaloreans love to buy. They also have heavy lehengas, as does Koskii across the street.

For men, Mahanta or Manyavar have the full set—kurta, headwear, footwear. Some of their kurtas are too 'jaal' or shiny, but they are good for emergencies. Go to Ramraj Cotton for half-sleeved white-shirts to wear over traditional silk dhotis (veshtis) for men. If you want to stitch men's kurtas, go to Manoranjan fabrics for lovely chikankari and other fabrics. You can buy yards of these fabrics and get it stitched by the tailors in Commercial Street. I have a network of tailors I use but if you ask in the stores, they will also recommend tailors.

For wedding card invitations, I have used Templetree run by Sonali Maniar and have been happy. Friends suggest going to Sultanpet and walking the streets for rows of stationery shops which can make wedding invitations. One friend has used Kamal Paper Corporation—look it up, it is in Sulthanpete—for her daughter's wedding invitations.

Jewellery is a tough one because it depends on if you like gemstones or not. Valanda is a jewellery studio owned by Chitra Pathi, who is an old Bangalorean. Find her on Instagram. Gujjadi Swarna Jewellers is an old jewellery brand. Lots of folks walk on Dickenson Road where every Kerala jeweller has a showroom. If you want to get your old jewellery valued, I recommend Tanishq (disclosure: I did some content work for them). They have a machine which will weigh your gold and also tell you what percentage of gold is present in each piece. I recently did this and was shocked to find that the bangles I inherited from my grandmother had only 75 per cent gold in them while the more recent pieces I acquired had over 90 per cent gold—which means purer. CKC has showrooms in central Bangalore and they are a brand where my Bangalore-based aunt buys all her jewellery—even though the family is now feuding. Ganjam is a brand I respect because Mr Umesh Ganjam has a sensibility that is unique.

Wedding decorations are another area where Bangalore excels. Just walk down Avenue Road or Jayanagar 4th Block market for 'seer' items which are decorative and placed on the dais. You can find 'sakkarai bommai' or sugar-made edible colourful dolls, designed cobre or coconut copras, and other fantastic objects.

Aayana Dance company is Bangalore-based and specializes in wedding dances. They do specific choreographies for walking the bride and groom in, and also perform for guests. Find them in Instagram and watch their showreels to see if their style works for you.

Like I said, this is a start. I have asked several Bangalore friends for their recommendations and if I manage to compile more 'helpful wedding shopping hints', I will share them here in the future.

∞

How to talk to your therapist: Bangalore's take on Jung

The festive season is here and there is a lot of feasting going on at my home. This is also the time when I take stock. I decide if I need a facial or should go on a juice cleanse to properly fit into Diwali clothes. I also look inside and wonder if that last huge fight I had with my husband was worth the pain. Like many folks, I speak about this to my therapist.

For the last decade, three areas have dominated my life: psychology, mythology and nature. I have an undergraduate degree in psychology. Since then, I have been studying the work of Carl Jung through online courses. I have worked with Jungian therapists for years. I keep a dream journal.

I like Carl Jung's analytical psychology because I feel that it is 'Eastern'-oriented with its emphasis on myths, dreams, symbols and archetypes. When Jung came to India, he said, 'Life in India has not yet withdrawn into the capsule of the head. It is the whole body that lives. No wonder the European feels dreamlike… When you walk with naked feet, how can you ever forget the earth?'

Nature is central to India's civilizational ethos. It is central to our faith, festivals, mythology and iconography. A composite sea creature called the makara guards the entrance of Hindu temples. There are sacred forests, sacred rivers, sacred mountains (the Himalayas are abodes of the Gods), gift-giving cows (Kamadhenu), self-eating beasts (kirtimukha), serpent gods (nagas), soaring protective birds (garuda). Even Hindu gods have elephant heads.

Hinduism is a polytheistic religion whose roots in animism and nature worship have not been cut off. We worship the sun, moon, stars and planets. We offer food to crows since they are supposed to carry the spirits of our ancestors. We hug and worship trees. We believe that cows contain 108 gods within them. We use rice flour to create rangoli-drawings outside our homes so that the ants can feed on them. Every aspect of Indian culture is linked to nature, even today.

However, there is one area in which Indian culture has not made what seems like an obvious connection to me. There is one field in which its religious myths, symbols and metaphors have not been explored as deeply, and that is psychology. This is where Carl Jung comes in.

Carl Jung's approach to psychology was holistic. It included spirituality, religion, mysticism and art. He was curious about 'primitive' thought and absorbed influences as varied as alchemy, the i-ching and mandala drawings. He travelled to Africa, to America to meet the Pueblo Indians of New Mexico, and finally to India. In every place, he moved away from civilized areas to absorb rural local cultures that lived close to the land. In 1939, Jung wrote an article 'What India can teach us', and praised its integrative approach to the self. India, Jung said, had avoided the 'fatal dissociation between an upper and a lower half of the human personality.' In other words, we Indians still retain the connection between head and heart, between the masculine and feminine aspects of ourselves. More than other cultures, we are 'whole' in the Jungian sense of the term.

India, like Europe, Egypt and China, is an old culture with a different way of looking at life: one that is anchored by its geography and history. Modern Indians know Hindu mythology, but they don't see a link between our stories and our psyche. Western psychology, particularly Jungian thought, has done a great deal to connect Greek and Roman myths, such as those involving the Goddess Psyche, Eros, Zeus and Apollo, to modern lives and thought. Jungian psychologists are able to connect mental health with mythology. But the myths that they draw from are mostly European. I would like to change this.

Hinduism is a deeply experiential faith that links emotions with the psyche. For example, a foundational story in Hinduism is the 'Churning of the Ocean'. The story is fantastic. The Gods and demons want the nectar of immortality. The only way is to churn the ocean using Mt Mandara turned upside down. A giant serpent, Vasuki, is used as the rope and a tortoise holds the mountain up so it doesn't sink. As the ocean is churned, a series of objects come up: first a mythic poison, then a white elephant, then the moon, a wish-fulfilling tree, then Kamadhenu, then Mohini...and so it goes.

When I look at this story through the lens of analytical

psychology (another name for Jungian psychology), there are so many possibilities. The ocean could represent our unconscious. The poison could represent what Jung called our 'shadow'. Each aspect of this story offers rich layers of meaning that can help practitioners of psychoanalysis understand Eastern myths and their place in the 'collective unconscious' of our species. Underneath it all, we are all humans after all.

So this festive season, among the many friends I visit, I also plan for another place that I will go to. Bangalore's Society of Analytical Psychology is planning a workshop on dreams. I plan to attend it so that I can explore a place that I visit often at night but seldom understand: my dreams.

∞

Civic duty Bangalore-ishtyle: Independence Day in Indiranagar

It is that time of year again when all of us engage in a healthy dose of nostalgia, amnesia and hope about how India has changed since Independence. Lists will come aplenty about things to be proud of and things to worry about. For this column though, I thought I would take a different tack. I thought I would figure out what I could do to help my community, city and therefore country: a small project that was doable.

If you ask city activists, philanthropists and evangelists about one issue that will give maximum bang for the buck in terms of helping Bengaluru, you will come up with many different answers, but two will likely top the list. One is a robust public transport system that will ease our city's traffic woes, and the second will likely have to do with infrastructure. To put this theory to test, I asked V. Ravichandar, who calls himself 'the patron saint of lost causes' and has worked across the public and private arena in Bangalore. What would help Bangalore the most? 'The challenge for our city projects is that the ideas are poorly conceived and therefore badly implemented,' he said. 'I would use philanthropic money to develop smart solutions that the city could implement with tax money to make life better for all of us.' What this meant was that the government ought to use the abundance of talent available in the city to come up with 'detailed project reports' before implementing the 'request for tender' protocol for civic solutions.

My takeaway from this was that it would be hard to do anything substantial in Bengaluru or any other city without government involvement. But what project could I tackle? I was mulling this when I got an invitation to the release of the 'Dorekere Biodiversity Report', at Gandhi Bhavan (or Gandhi Bhavana, as it is called in Karnataka, where we elongate the last letter of each word). I came away inspired because it is a stellar example of how citizens take charge of a lake, use the help of government and other civic bodies such as the Public Works Department (PWD), BBMP and others in order to rejuvenate said lake—or at least prevent it from deteriorating. Bengaluru used to be a city of lakes. Estimates vary but there used to be at least 270 lakes. Now there are about 80 living lakes in Bengaluru.

I live in Ulsoor near Ulsoor Lake. The lake is dead. It used to be alive but these days, thanks to copious sewage water from apartment buildings being released into the lake, life has no chance. From what I understood, in order to rejuvenate a lake, you need a whole range of what the corporate world calls 'stakeholders'. So I decided to get buy-in from all my neighbouring apartment complexes by throwing a party.

Okay, let us leave out the Ambani wedding—about which enough has been said. Let us just think of parties in the normal sense of the term, not in terms of pre- and post-wedding parties where global superstars show up. In terms of throwing parties, I thought (and still think) that Delhi does it best, and not only because the rich folks in Delhi have space—think of those bungalows in Lutyens' Delhi with sprawling lawns. Plus, Delhi has the natural flamboyance that comes from the Punjabi influence—the 'show off' culture that my Delhi friends mock.

Bengaluru and Chennai are hamstrung by their southern notions of the evil eye and the concept of 'enough', which means that you cannot think of gaudy grandiose show-off parties. Hyderabad did not fall prey to this culture of 'enough' and these days, most Kerala cities with their love of gold also have no qualms in showing off. Haven't you seen photos and reels of Kerala weddings where the bride wears enough gold necklaces that they become a gold armour?

Bengaluru is changing though and these days, here too, you see parties that are not necessarily the obviously 'show off' variety, but don't skimp on the flamboyance either. The great news in Bengaluru is that if you want to enjoy a party, there are many ways of doing this. Organizing a party or event is equal parts love, equal parts sharing, and equal parts agenda. And my agenda with this party was clear: I needed people who would help me clean Ulsoor Lake. I needed Kannada speakers who could work with the BBMP to stop the sewage, researchers who knew how to rejuvenate this dead lake, naturalists who could teach us residents how to attract migrating birds, and philanthropists to fund the whole thing. The great thing is that you throw in a few beers and a lot of neighbourly conversation, and the whole thing falls in place. Within an evening, we had a group of citizens interested in lake preservation and restoration. And now the real work begins. I will keep you posted.

❧

What kids carry to college: Health faucets and Maggi noodles

Right about now, hundreds of thousands of students all over India will be leaving home for college. For parents, this means confronting the 'university list' of things that you should pack for your offspring. The best list that I have seen so far is from the Dhirubhai Ambani School in Mumbai. It includes brilliant things like a portable bidet. The Indian health faucet is a hugely underrated item. Until I learned of this handheld portable health faucet, I had resigned myself to using inferior tissue papers for my, ahem, morning ablutions. Not anymore. Not only have I bought this portable bidet for my offspring, but I also have 10 extra ones to gift to every kid going abroad for education. My grandfather used to travel with a portable enema, but the bidet is much more practical and user-friendly. It is available online. Look for one where the spray is strong.

The other things that are included in most college packing lists are 'samaham sachets' for cold and cough. I had no idea that such a thing existed but after trying it out, I added it to my travel list alongside Vicks VapoRub and Amrit Dhara pearls for indigestion.

The food item that does not seem to make many college lists is Maggi noodles, probably because it may be full of questionable substances that better parents don't feed their children. It is a beloved comfort food for my kids. Indeed, the Ambani 'university list' did not have a single food item, which I found odd, having bought enough MTR powders and Bukhara instant foods to fill a suitcase. A wise Mumbai friend explained this void. 'We in Mumbai vacuum-pack fresh foods and theplas from Chheda stores and send it weekly to our children,' she said. And then we wonder why our kids are not growing up to be independent adults.

Did our parents take so much trouble when we pushed off to college? I doubt it but then, that is the creation story that every generation tells itself. 'When I went to college, my parents didn't even come to drop me off. My father didn't even know what subjects I was studying. I didn't even attend my graduation—got my degree by mail. And now, we are celebrating kindergarten graduations.' Are we envious or proud by these developments?

There are some objects, however, whose utility is ten times their size. I would submit the humble safety pin as the Swiss army knife of packing for Indian women. I use the safety pin to pop out my SIM card from iPhones, pin and tuck the sari, and draw a bindi with black kajal at a pinch. I also used the closed safety pin to clean my ears but would not recommend it.

There are two kinds of people in the world: those who can pack and those who cannot. It has nothing to do with meticulousness or organization. I know a doctor who keeps meticulous records and runs a superbly organized clinic. Put him in front of a suitcase and he gets anxious. He doesn't travel much and therefore doesn't have much practice with packing.

My packing issues run much deeper and have to do with choice. There is a term in computer science called binary tree. It talks about a data structure in which each 'node' has two child nodes, called 'siblings' and 'ancestors'. My packing binary tree bifurcates endlessly between sibling and ancestor. For every item of clothing, I have questions, which lead to more questions. Should I wear this in the morning or in the evening? If evening, should I pack it right away or leave it out as a last choice? If last choice, will I remember it? Since the question tree never resolves, my entire packing exercise remains stalled.

For college students, packing is about applying scenarios. Take out a shirt and figure out which part of your college schedule would suit it—pun intended. Slot specific objects to specific times and events. Work forwards, then work backwards, then give up and let your parent do the packing.

In a TED talk, psychologist Barry Schwartz gave a lecture on the paradox of choice. Having too many choices, he said, stymied action. You walk into a grocery store and see an endless array of cereals and are not sure what to buy. Having a plethora of blue jeans when you need just one cripples the process. The same applies to packing. The problem for our children is one of plenty. They have too many 'essentials' and we pack too many 'necessities' for them. As proof, I submit the acupuncture cushion I gave my daughter to encourage her to sit cross-legged on the ground to study, rather than sprawling on the bed. It was never used.

The best part of the Ambani packing list was the 'vasthu' section which said that the study table ought to face northeast (governed by the lord of wealth, Kubera). As with feng shui or vasthu, there are loopholes which involve fish-tanks and mirrors. The college bed is to face south or east. If not, get your kid to symbolically lie down in that direction before sleeping. And lastly put family photos in the southeast corner per vasthu. If there is no wall in the southeast corner, suspend photos from the ceiling in that location.

I have great respect for those kids who will allow their parents to rejig their rooms through vasthu principles, and am totally envious of parents who have brought up such kids who will listen to them on any matter, let alone vasthu. As for me, the best I can do is move my own desk to the northeast corner and hope that my kids will not eat Maggi every night.

Self-Care with Dr Shetty: How to take care of yourself in 2025

Today is officially the start of resolution season. You know what I mean. We have eaten more Diwali sweets and Christmas cake than is good for us. Time to stop, we tell ourselves. Time to take charge of our health, habits and goals. The question is how.

I subscribe to many fitness podcasts, read self-help books, and follow a routine that is based on convenience rather than medical advice. So imagine my delight when I heard two actionable items from Dr Devi Shetty, the eminent cardiac surgeon. Dr. Shetty was talking about diabetes—rampant in India—and how HbA1C was a marker for longevity. 'When you are in your eighties, the one marker that will define the quality of your future life is your HbA1C levels,' he said. So keeping sugar levels in check is something that all of us need to do. How to do this? 'Don't stop eating sweets,' he advised. "Instead put a small piece of sweet into your mouth and keep it there. Let it take its time and melt. This will tell the neurotransmitters in the brain that they are satiated.' The other thing Dr Shetty talked about was timed walks. 'After each meal, take a 15-minute walk,' he tells patients with diabetes. 'That's like getting an insulin shot.'

So there you are. Two actionable items. Savour a piece of sweet and take a walk after each meal. Each one of us can do that. Keeping the habit is difficult though. I discover this when I visit Radha Krishnaswamy, a functional strength trainer in Indiranagar. I am there for an analysis of my posture, pain, gait and pronation. Over the course of an hour, Radha takes photos of how I stand, squat, lunge, lift my arms and move my legs. I discover that I am involuntarily leaning right. I also learn that my thighs and core need strengthening. Radha suggests simple exercises for correction. For example, stand on one leg and shut your eyes. Try it. You will be shocked at how much you wobble. 'As you get older, you need to focus on balance and reflexes so that you can prevent falls or learn to fall better,' says Radha. Standing on one foot with eyes closed helps with both.

My brother and I used to tell each other that our Dad was a 'good faller', in that he seemed to know how to fall so that he didn't break bones. In his eighties, Appa used to fall and each time he got wounds and gashes but thankfully no broken bones. Learning to fall is a lot about reflexes. Thankfully there are exercises each of us can do to fall better. For women, addressing knee pain is a big issue. Radha suggests Kegel exercises as a way to identify and improve core muscles. First you do this while sitting, then while exercising, so that you use core muscles to lift and flex.

Most of us focus so much on activity that we don't

pay attention to how we stand, sit or move. Ergonomics and posture are a big part of how we hold our body and move, and the reason for much of the pains that each of us develops. In Bangalore, there are several practitioners of somatic therapies. Dr Deepak Sharan, an orthopaedic surgeon who founded Recoup Health, is someone who combines medical training with somatic practices—he has certifications in the Feldenkrais method, Alexander technique, the DART procedures, the Franklin method and ergonomics. According to him, there are several reasons why we feel discomfort and pain. 'We expend too much energy and effort while doing simple movements (like getting out of a chair). We don't have good self-awareness while moving. We don't know how our body is organized and positioned—certain areas are tight or bent, and so on.' The other reason has to do with compensations our body makes due to past injuries. Somatic practices help you realign and readjust the body to heal pain and prevent injuries. All these begin with body awareness or proprioception.

So here are some specific movement practices that I am doing in 2025. Multiplanar movement is a fancy word for movement that involves moving forward, sideways and backwards. I try to walk sidewards within my house and climb backwards up and down the stairs. Multilateral movement involves using limbs that move in different directions. This sounds complex but the movement of our hands when we walk is a multilateral movement. Reduce the tension in your neck and shoulders consciously. Sigh deeply. Be aware of jaw tightness. Take pleasure in movement by doing things slowly, like in tai chi. Stay still, like in yoga. Breathe deeply when possible. Loosen and lengthen your spine by imagining your neck floating upwards. Becoming aware of and improving how you move through your day may be the best New Year's gift you can give to yourself.

What do you tell your loved ones?

It has just been a couple of months since the New Year and I have attended two weddings and two funerals already. Since they happened one after the other, I have put them together in my mind: love and death, and how the two are connected.

An uncle passed away. At his funeral and on the subsequent days, I witnessed an outpouring of love from his family, relatives, people he mentored and neighbours. They spoke of him with affection and admiration. All of them said the same few things: about his uncommon kindness, curiosity about the world, his ability to treat politicians and peons with the same respect, and his love for words, travel and food. All of which led me to wonder about the age-old question: what will your obituary say? What will people say about you after you are gone? What will they speak about at your memorial service? Which is another way of asking: who are you and what do you project to the world?

Having been in the depressing position of attending a few funerals recently, I find that career matters less than character when it comes to what people remember about you—unless you happened to have developed a game-changing business, invention, or framework. Most memorial services speak about core values that are essential to being human—about kindness, affection, warmth, a sense of humour, about being optimistic, having high integrity, about being helpful and empathetic. These are outer-focused traits however. Each of us has something unique and wacky about who we are. The beauty of getting old is that most elders I know embrace their eccentricities. They have long given up trying to put on their 'game-face' for the outer world. They don't try to be who they are not. Age and inability have put paid to their desire to live for others. Now they are just quirky, whacky, stubborn old folks who have individual desires and penchants—whether it is doing the crossword puzzle, or peeling a pomegranate just so. The reason visiting an elder is oddly calming is because in them you see who you are not. In them, you see a person who exudes authenticity effortlessly, not because they are trying to but because they have stopped trying to do what the world asks them to.

The question is whether you can shortcut this. Can you be authentic when in your forties, fifties and sixties instead of waiting till you are in your eighties to do this? I don't think so, because early in life, you are enmeshed in roles and duties. You are a sibling, parent, child, spouse and colleague, all at the same time. Each role demands something different, and each situation demands a different code of behaviour. There are very few people who are in outward-facing positions who are able to follow Shakespeare's dictum in Hamlet: 'To thine own self be true.'

Easy to say, Polonius, but if I did this, my world would explode. I have to hold my tongue with kids, spouse, sibling, parents, friends and colleagues. It is called politeness and telling white lies, and both of these lubricate life.

Recently, though, I had a different sort of epiphany. Perhaps it was the funerals that I was attending. 'I think I should tell my mother what she means to me,' I told my husband. 'And maybe you should too, either by writing a letter or making a recording that she can play.'

'That's not my way,' he replied. 'My way is to give them small moments of joy.'

The larger question though is whether your loved ones know how much you love them. I think in today's age we tend to shower love and praise on our children. But have you told your parent recently about how much they mean to you? How? Certainly, my parents are not of the generation where public display of affection was common. My mother, for example, has never used the phrase 'I love you'. But I feel the strength of her love almost every day, even though she is frail at 86. It shows up in weird ways. When I tell her that I have to write an article on sarees, she will ask the next person she meets—in my presence—about sarees. 'Shoba is writing about sarees. Do you have any ideas?' she will ask the housekeeper of my building as we walk together. Is this love? Is this what is called 'enabling' your children? I feel so.

We have just had Valentine's Day. Holi is coming up. Both celebrate love, which most of us associate with the romance that we have with partners and spouses. But maybe we also need to figure out how to express our love to the folks we take for granted: our parents.

How organizations fail to include

Shailaja Paik's Wikipedia page does not mention that she grew up in the slums around Pune. It does mention that she is the winner of the 2024 MacArthur 'genius' grant. Shailaja is a historian of modern India who focuses on the intersections of class, sexuality and caste. 'I wanted to connect with women who I wanted to study,' says Shailaja on MacArthur Foundation's YouTube channel. 'But to write and to understand the stories of the marginalized, the excluded, you need a different method.'

The same could be said of the organization that awarded her this hefty $800,000 grant paid out over five years. In the early years after its institution in 1981, the MacArthur grants were heavily skewed in favour of white men. A study tracking inclusiveness in the fellowships found that 63 per cent of the awardees were male between 1981 and 2018.* Around 2018, a host of grant-

*Kaba, A.J., 'MacArthur Fellows, 1981–2018: Gender, Race and Educational Attainment', *Sociology Mind, 10,* 2020, https://tinyurl.com/sasc6w2h. Accessed on 3 September 2025.

giving foundations in America including the MacArthur and the Guggenheim announced that they were going to make a conscious effort to be inclusive. Since then, women dominate the MacArthur grant list. Every year, at least 50 per cent (and usually more) of the grants go to women. This year, for instance, 12 out of 22 Fellows are women. The same applies to the Guggenheim Fellowships. In recent years, close to 50 per cent of the grants are awarded to women.

How did the MacArthur Foundation with an annual budget of about $160 million, a staff of around 250 people and a jury of about a dozen, become so spectacularly inclusive not just in terms of gender parity but also in every other domain? The answer is both obvious and very hard to achieve: by acknowledging their bias, and actively seeking to overcome it. Consider the DEI (Diversity, Equity and Inclusion) Commitment that the MacArthur has written out. It begins with humility, acknowledges historical biases, and clearly lists out steps that the organization is taking to overcome it. A lot of it has to do with the composition of leadership, staff and the jury. It is no coincidence that Marlies Carruth, the director of the MacArthur Fellows, took up her role in 2021. She happens to be a woman of colour.

Inclusion matters, not because it is nice to have but because in today's world, it is vital to have diverse voices who speak in rainbow tongues and tones. If you have a small jury of folks who speak in the same rational tongue, without scope for challenge, then you end up in the same spot that most mature foundations were in their early years—where they said they were just and fair, when in fact they were largely giving prizes, awards and fellowships to men who looked and spoke like them. The minute a jury starts talking about the 'right fit' and 'appropriate' topics, you know that they are going to be safe rather than inclusive. Not that you need to burn the house down in order to include more women. Quite the opposite.

In August 2020, the Guggenheim took several steps including sending its 200 staff members on a 'listening tour' to ensure inclusion in its grants and awards. Its document emphasizes specific steps but also uses data to ensure accountability. Essentially, the organization changed their framework.

Bangalore has a number of organizations that are in the business of promoting scholarship, either through grants, conferences, awards or fellowships. Each of them states that they espouse and promote excellence. Perhaps they do. But the way this is done, the way money is disbursed does not reflect values of parity and equity along with excellence—and we have just seen that this is possible, at least in America.

To be just and equitable requires courage and a force of will. It requires actively seeking out diversity—in the leadership and in jury composition. Every time I speak about this topic with men, they punt the problem and solution back at me. They have the same tired response: we try our best to be fair, but there just aren't enough women of merit. Really? They tell me to offer suggestions to correct the situation. Sure, our keynote speakers are disproportionately male, they will say. Why don't you supply a list of good women candidates? This approach assumes that gender is a woman's issue and that equity is an accommodation that men make towards including women. To be inclusive is to enlarge the spectrum of what is possible. It opens your mind.

To value justice and parity requires leaders of organizations to change how they think. It requires that they first acknowledge that every jury and every board is biased. The best way to correct bias is to hire more women at every level: in the staff, leadership, board and juries. Why did it take Shailaja Paik to go to America to be acknowledged as a genius? More crucially to India, how many Shailajas are organizations failing to spot, fund and promote?

Today, both the MacArthur and the Guggenheim are headed by women. Their staff composition and the recipients of their prestigious grants and awards reflect the parity that these organizations espouse and aspire towards. The effects of this parity will be visible only years later, but for now, what a glorious world it is for the young women who aspire to be 'geniuses'.

Pity this is not happening in India.

Prayer and pollution: The Bengaluru balancing act

The Kumbh is coming to Bengaluru, or at least a version of it. On 21 March, we are having a Cauvery Aarthi in Sankey Tank, complete with priests from UP who will conduct it. Heralded as a 'first-ever' religious spectacle that honours the Cauvery river, this event is the brain-child of the Bengaluru Water Supply and Sewerage Board (BWSSB), which, along with the BBMP, is pretty much the go-to for anything in this ill-regulated city. However, Dr V. Ram Prasath Manohar, who was appointed to be the head of the BWSSB last year, seems to be a man who is ambitious, foolhardy or both. He is the convener of the Friends of Lakes collective, and has released statements saying that he hopes that spiritual initiatives such as the Cauvery Aarthi will inspire authorities to take stricter measures to prevent lake pollution. But he is the ultimate authority of Bangalore's water bodies. The challenge he poses is directed at himself. What is he going to do?

Last week, I read that the BWSSB and the BBMP were

'improving' Ulsoor Lake, which is in my neighbourhood. The problem with such improvements is that they mostly involve fat construction contracts to build more cement sidewalks and embankments, all of which will drive away the lake shore-birds that depend on gradual depths in which they can stand and catch fish. What really needs to happen in all of Bengaluru's lakes is sewage removal, which is a Herculean task. My building along with many others that border Ulsoor Lake are prime culprits. It is our sewage that goes into the lake. So, in a sense I am both culprit and well-wisher of this particular waterbody.

Manohar's idea to create the Kaveri (or Cauvery) Aarthi in Sankey Tank is an idea fraught with problems. Who will remove the garbage post the event? Will Sankey Tank get more clogged up after thousands throw flowers and diyas into it? Will the BWSSB and the BBMP work together to get the site back into shape after the spectacle? Or will the citizens have to step in and do the heavy-lifting, as always?

Bengaluru has always been a city where citizens want to participate in the city's improvement only to be rebuffed by the government. Several organizations like Janaagraha, Bangalore Political Action Committee, Oorvani, Cubbon Park Canines, and Sensing Local have worked for years to improve the city's governance. Other organizations like Atta Galatta, Bangalore International Centre and Sabha do their bit to enhance their neighbourhood.

Sabha is the newest one. It is a heritage restoration project—spearheaded by Hema and V. Ravichander—that took an old architectural structure and repurposed it sensitively, thanks to architect Bijoy Ramachandran of A Hundred Hands. Since its opening last year, Sabha has hosted music concerts, talks, and other events such as a pop-up of Kayastha cuisine from Lucknow and Hyderabad created by textile enthusiast Manish Saxena.

I have attended a few pop-ups recently. The Oberoi had a Thai pop-up of the Michelin-starred Bo.Lan from Bangkok. What was interesting was that even though the flavours were Thai, they were very different from the food that I normally taste at Rim Naam. The Ritz-Carlton's all-day dining restaurant, Market, has decided to go a la carte for dinner. I attended a preview hosted by Reuben Katarian, the general manager. When I asked him what it took to change the format of a restaurant, he said 'Courage', which is a good answer because the stakes are high when big ships change course.

Bengaluru is full of bar takeovers and restaurant pop-ups. These are usually great because they bring the world to our city. But I find that Indians these days are interested in deep-dives into our own wonderful cuisines. One restaurant talked about doing a restaurant pop-up that combined the attars of Kannauj with food. To me, this seems like a great idea. There are so many other combinations that make sense in our syncretic country—connecting food with flowers, fragrance, textiles, festivals, music and dance. This type of immersive experience is what we all call 'next level'. It elevates the food and the experience.

The only problem is time commitment. Every pop-up I have been to takes three hours and this is more time than any of us have. I think restaurants who plan on doing pop-ups ought to give themselves 1.5 hours per menu. This is how we eat in India: where a thali with everything lets us pick and choose what and how we want to eat and in which order. The course-by-course experience is wonderful if the pacing is perky. Otherwise, you just sit around and wait for the next course and get more full and dispirited as the afternoon or evening wears on.

Akhila Srinivas who runs The Courtyard arguably runs one of the most interesting dining spaces in the city, partly because its premise is pop-ups. I have been there several times and—except for parking—it has always been a welcoming and warm space. And thankfully, it doesn't take three hours per dining experience.

Beyond startups to pop-ups: Bangalore's new hustle

Akhila Srinivas may well be Bangalore's queen of pop-ups. Akhila runs The Courtyard, her family home now transformed into a gathering space, and The Conservatory, which has hosted a number of restaurant pop-ups that are not as expensive as the five-star ones but aren't cheap either (the range is from ₹1,500 to ₹6,000 per person per meal). What distinguishes her curations is that they are rooted in a specific cuisine prepared in a specific way. Consider the recent line-up: Sienna Café's Bengali food, Gingko Pune's Uzuki summer menu, the Maratha Kitchen's food, and more. There are a lot of women chefs with interesting takes on their native and learned food, be it Goan or Keralite. A good indication of their popularity is that five-star chefs get on the wait-list to attend. So what's the feedback, I asked Akhila. 'Visiting chefs say that Bangalore's diners are both adventurous and attentive to food,' she says. 'When a chef comes to explain the concept, the diners actually listen.'

At the other end of the spectrum is the recently

finished culinary pop-up at The Leela Palace Bengaluru with 3 Michelin-starred Chef Massimo Bottura. Priced at ₹50,000+ per person, the sold-out event attracted visitors from Bangalore and nearby cities who don't hesitate to spend for high-end experiences brought to their doorstep. Bangalore à la Delhi, you might say.

I think of all this as I talk to Raihan Vadra, during the Bangalore Art Weekend that happened last month. Raihan is 25 and together with *Svasa Life* magazine, *Platform Magazine*, The Usual Suspects India community, brand-agency Form & Flow and other collaborators, he put together a weekend of panel discussions, art, music and fashion, all held at Sabha, a restored bungalow in Kamaraj Road. I try not to bring up his mother, Priyanka, and his father, Robert, both of whom have been in the news. Instead, I ask the Delhi-based visual artist about how Bangalore is different from the events that he has organized in Delhi and Mumbai.

Well, for one thing, Bangaloreans actually listen, he replies, echoing what Akhila said. In Delhi, young people quickly lose interest in hour-long panel-discussions. In Bangalore, as I witnessed, there were panel discussions held over two days, on topics ranging from conscious living to making films. A full house of people mostly in their 20s and 30s sat patiently and listened. The second thing Raihan mentioned was the fact that the entire weekend was alcohol-free, which would be unheard of in Delhi. Kombucha was on offer from Dad's Hack, created by Bangalore boy Zeshan Rahaman. But the sessions were still packed with folks, chatting and viewing art. In Delhi, said Raihan, unless it is a 'party', meaning unless there is alcohol, it is hard to get folks to attend. The last thing he mentioned was that there seemed to be a 'hunger for art and culture' here in Bangalore. Now this is something that feels contradictory. On the one hand, talk to art galleries like Sakshi and Sumukha and they will say that Bangaloreans don't buy, or appreciate, art. We may have our startup billionaires but culture, we lack. Even Chennai buys more art, they will say. But that may refer to older folks who have the means to buy fine art. The youth of Bangalore have a hunger for other forms of culture including zines (self-made magazines), graphic art and manga.

Bangalore Art Weekend was nominally about art, but it also had workshops on zine-making, sketching and design. The panel discussions were on subjects such as performance poetry, ad films, reclaiming public spaces, mental health, upcycling of clothes, getting off social media, and living a slower, more intentional life. Designers sold clothes. But most importantly, people stayed back to listen.

My favourite recent pop-up was an exhibition of embroidery artworks by ten Lambadi artisans who undertook a residency under the guidance of Bangalore-based fashion designer Anshu Arora, who along with her husband, Jason Cherian, founded a label called The Small Shop. Anshu connected with The Porgai Artisans Association where over 60 women who belong to the Lambadi tribe relearned the embroidery techniques that was their heritage. What Anshu did over a four-month residency was nudge them into making embroidery art so that it could be elevated to gallery spaces and command a lot more money. Ten women volunteered and created a stunning variety of artworks that were sold in Sabha. I attended a panel discussion on the last day in which the visionary founder of Tribal Health Initiative (under which Porgai operates) Dr. Lalitha Regi spoke about how crafts such as the Lambadi embroidery could be brought back from the brink of disappearance. As I stood and gazed at the intricate embroidery panels hung in the museum-like space, I felt as if I were in the beautiful Sittilingi Valley where these women live and work among birds, bees, trees and butterflies.

Why Bangaloreans love lakes

Recently, I attended the premiere of *My Otter Diary*, a film by acclaimed wildlife filmmaker and National Geographic Fellow Sugandhi Gadadhar and her producer-husband Rana (Raghunath) Belur. Filmed over five years, it explores the symbiotic relationship between otters and the river Kaveri. Otters, says Sugandhi, are to the river what tigers are to a jungle: they are apex predators who preserve and enhance the ecosystem that they belong to.

The screening was held at Shankar Nag theatre in M.G. Road and the entire wildlife community was in attendance. Through the film, I got to know the river Kaveri in all her glory. Kaveri looms large in the minds of this city and state. For Kodavas in particular, Kaveri is their home and reigning patron goddess. Which made me wonder, is it because of the river Kaveri that Bangaloreans love their lakes so much? Lots of things fail in civic activism in our city, but stray dogs and lake restoration command passion; witness the rejuvenation of Puttanahalli lake and others. Why do Bangaloreans love their lakes so much?

Architect Naresh Narasimhan has a nifty narrative to explain this. He says that Bangalore is perhaps the only large city in the world that has developed on a plateau with nary a natural object nearby. Most civilizations were established beside rivers. Ditto for large cities of the world: the river Seine flows through Paris, the Hudson through New York, and the Nile through many great African cities. Bangalore, on the other hand, became a city because it was at the crossroads of trade routes. This is why, says Naresh, the old city area or Pete (pronounced pay-tay) is full of trading communities including Marwaris, Settys and Mudaliars. To protect the Pete, Bangalore's erstwhile rulers built a kote (ko-tay) or fort. Once Bangalore thrived, the rulers began building *thotta*s or gardens including Lal Bagh and Cubbon Park. In order to water the gardens, they established lakes or *kere*s. This nifty pete-kotte-thotta-kere model of Bangalore's development is something Naresh speaks about often. Bangaloreans love lakes because we built them. They are all man-made with bunds holding the water in, and sluices to connect one to the other.

Civic evangelist V. Ravichander quotes the legend of Kempe Gowda as an additional reason. The story goes that when Kempe Gowda decided to establish his dream city on the plateau with hillocks where Bangalore exists today, his mother is supposed to have told him: 'Keregalum kattu, maragalum nadu' (build lakes, plant trees). Kempe Gowda did just that, building hundreds of lakes and gardens.

By some accounts, Bangalore used to be a city of a thousand lakes—one crowdsourced initiative put it at 1,521 lakes. What is more reasonable is that we used to have some 280 lakes, of which only 80 currently remain under the ambit of the BBMP. Even calling them lakes is a misnomer. In an evocative 2014 paper by Professor Meera Baindur, titled 'Bangalore Lake story: reflections on the spirit of a place',* she talks about a holy man who used to come and sit under a tree beside a kere to conduct rites and rituals. This tight and daily connection that Bangalore's early people had with the kere in their neighbourhood does not exist anymore. In public presentations and in paper, researcher Rohan D'Souza has stated that a kere refers to an ecosystem rather than a mere water body. It is literally larger than life in the Kannada imagination.

The good news is that Bangalore's keres are slowly making a comeback, thanks mostly to RWAs that have taken it upon themselves to improve the ecosystem. The worst time for our lakes was in February 2017 when Bellandur Lake caught fire, thanks to the large amount of toxic waste released into it. Cut to 2022 when the 'Lakeman of India', a Bangalore resident Anand Malligavad, helped to restore Kyalasanahalli Kere. As an aside, let me ask if part of the problem is the fact that most of these lakes have long, barely pronounceable names?

Malligavad, even today, continues to be at the forefront of lake restoration. D'Souza documents how government bodies treat water bodies such as Rachenahalli Kere, thus making them accountable.** Civic activism has also kept

---

*Baindur, Meera, 'Bangalore Lake Story: Reflections on the Spirit of a Place', *Journal of Cultural Geography*, Informa UK Limited, 2014.

**D'Souza, Rohan, 'Rachenahalli – Containment of a Kere – A Visual Essay', Reflections, 26 May 2014, https://tinyurl.com/ymdr2ywe. Accessed

real estate developers away from lakes, not always and not always successfully, but not for nothing either.

What next? As an immigrant to Bangalore, although one who has lived here now for nearly 20 years, I remain fascinated by the hold that these lakes have on the city's collective imagination. But in order for lakes to revive or even survive, people need to have a connection with it that goes beyond just morning walks. Unless people are able to relate to each kere as a living ecosystem that gives them something, why would you want to save it?

❧

---

on 3 September 2025.

The perfumers of Bangalore: Jasmine and sandalwood

I am standing at Al-Kareem Attars and Perfumes in Ibrahim Sahib Street, discussing Ruh Gulab with Maria, the woman behind the counter. It is evening but even though she has been sniffing all day, Maria says she doesn't get 'nose fatigue'. So we converse about what I want: a milder version of the classic Jannat-ul-firdaus or Garden of Paradise attar with floral and woody layers. Actually, I am told that *ittr*s are the correct name for the scents and attars are the perfumers who make them. When I searched for the right way to say 'maker of attars', it gave me 'baai uttri' as a choice, but since I don't speak Arabic, I am not sure.

Scents are a conversation. In Bangalore, Ally Mathan was and is the original perfumer, but since I live near Commercial Street, I end up visiting with the attar-perfumers there. The beauty of living in Bangalore or any other city in India is that you can discuss scents with perfumers to create unique fragrances that suit a moment and mood. Scents, after all, do what words cannot. They speak for you.

The scent of Bangalore is sandalwood and jasmine. To experience sandalwood, you have to drive two hours to Mysore, where the wood is distilled into small bottles that smell of the forest floor. The shortcut, of course, is that you can buy sandalwood essential oil at Cauvery Emporium on M.G. Road for a lot of money.

But what I am interested in these days is the rose. I have heard about the roses of Hassayan, outside Agra, from my perfumer friend, Jahnvi Lakhota Nandan. She told me that nearly four tonnes of damask or Noor Jehan roses are picked before sunrise 'by men and women moving like shadows', then sent to Kannauj in wicker baskets where they are distilled in large copper pots that are slowly heated. The hot steam releases the essential oils of the flower which then flows through bamboo pipes into another container. This is called the *ruh al gulab*, or 'soul of the rose'.

Indians and Arab cultures have a sophistication about perfume that is native and layered. We know how to use attars, pastes and unguents. In Bangalore, I can indulge in it by visiting one of the many attar shops in Shivaji Nagar. Ibrahim Sahib street is where I begin because it contains several attar shops including Al-Kareem, La Scents, IRS Perfume World, Ajmal, Asma Perfumery and other traditional attar stores that have now morphed to create perfumes that mimic Western scents from brands such as Roja Dove, Le Labo, Gucci and others.

Earlier, I used to choose these Western mimics, but now I gravitate towards traditional Arab scents. My current favourite is Mukhallat Jujur, a variation of the classic rose-oud combo that is the basis of many Arab perfumes. Mukhallat means blend, as opposed to classic ittrs where flowers, herbs and resins are distilled into a base of sandalwood oil: a Karnataka connection.

As I told photographer-filmmaker Ramya Reddy, who also creates perfumes for her brand, Coonoor & Co, smell is linked to identity and memory. A fragrance can take you to a lemon tree that you sampled as a teenager; to a childhood crush who smelled of musk; or to the vetiver root that protected you from the sun.

The mother of all scents of course is nature. The flint and minerality of her rocks is seen in Chablis wines. The smell of spices reminds all Indians of their grandmothers. It is in our poetry: wet earth and pouring rain, to quote from a Sangam poem, that reeks of petrichor. The jasmine-musk that Indians dab behind their ear lobes is both subtle and blatant. Inside each saree lies a thousand smells and stories, each wrapped in nostalgia. A scent, thus, connects your past, present and future. It moves you in ways that you cannot articulate or even fathom. Fragrance, like poetry, is emotion compressed into a bottle or verse.

The pleasure of buying *mukhallats* and ittrs in Shivaji Nagar is the fact that you can inhale the smells, adjust their notes, and see what they evoke and invoke. Each smell restores feelings that have been broken by the long arm of time. They carry jolts of imagination, for both perfumer and wearer. A rose can hit you with the force of a sledgehammer. But mix it with musk and it becomes a gentle santoor. A tuberose can confuse, but mix it with amber, and it sings. Scents, in that sense, take you home.

In Bangalore, there are several ways we experience perfume. One is through local incense brands like Sugandha Lok which has a shop in Gandhi Bazaar. The other is through fragrance oils. The last and perhaps the most labour-intensive is by wearing flower garlands in our hair. All these three traditions go back in time. Early Indian men used to adorn themselves with flowers too, by wearing garlands on bare chests, perfect attire for a tropical country like India. Sadly for men, that bare-chested garland-wearing tradition has been killed because we have copied western attire with all its prudishness.

The great news is that attars, ittrs (call it as you will) and mukhallats are accessible to all of us. So go ahead, buy that vial of mitti perfume, or green vetiver, or musk-rose, *champaka* or jasmine perfume. Put it on your pulse points. Guess what? The day will immediately start looking better.

Why Kannada deserves more than apologies

Let me just come out and say it: *Kannada-dalli maathadi.* Which is like saying, Hindi *mein baath kijiye.* Or *Tamizh-pesu.* I have chosen these three languages for a reason. Very recently, actor Kamal Haasan offered up a third instance of folks being caught in a Kannada-language controversy. The players may be different but the script is the same. Singer Sonu Nigam refused to sing a Kannada song in his Bangalore concert and later issued an apology. An SBI bank manager in Bangalore was caught on camera speaking in Hindi to a Kannada-speaking customer and then proclaiming that she would never learn Kannada. And now, Kamal Haasan said that Kannada was born from Tamil. All three, in their own way, have cast aspersions on the Kannada language which, by the way, boasts the largest number of Jnanpith awardees, save Hindi. It is also the only language besides Hindi in which an Indian author has won a Booker Prize: Geetanjali Shree and, more recently, Banu Mushtaq respectively.

Do Kannadigas have a chip on their shoulder about their native language? They didn't used to. I know North Indians who moved from Delhi to Bangalore 30 years ago and still don't speak a word of Kannada. These days, though, language tensions have taken over the state. We have auto-drivers who demand that their rides speak to them in Kannada. In the past year, vandals broke and removed signs in Central Bengaluru that did not have Kannada signage. The government had to issue a directive ordering signage that included Kannada, and now, all over the city you see signs written in the beautiful cursive of the Kannada language.

I moved to Bangalore nearly 20 years ago. I learned and now speak Kannada. It has opened the city to me in a way that would not be possible without speaking the local tongue. What befuddles me is that this has become a controversial issue rather than the norm. If a Kannadiga moves to Kanpur and speaks in Kannada rather than Hindi, do you think the local folks there would put up with it? Catch a Chennai auto-driver giving the time of day to anyone who doesn't speak Tamil, and I can say this because I grew up in Chennai. But Kannadigas are expected to speak in Hindi, Tamil, Telegu or whatever language is thrown at them. And you know what, they do, perhaps to their own detriment. That's the thing. Bangaloreans are by and large accepting, flexible, and multilingual. You have homes where Tamil, Kannada and Telegu are all spoken because this city lies in the crossroads of several states. This is why people from all over the world feel comfortable here. They have all been accommodated. Until now. What happened?

To paraphrase a famous historical speech, it has taken a while for the soul of the Kannadiga, long suppressed, to find utterance. To use the language of school bullies, the people of Karnataka have put up and shut up for a long time. Immigrants from all over India have populated their state and city without assimilating into their language or culture. Isn't language the real route to culture? Would this be possible in any other state or city? I doubt it. Then why should a Kannadiga put up with this?

I think it is about time the state and this city get their hackles up to safeguard their language. As someone who has learned it as an adult, I can tell you that it is not a difficult language. Immigrants come, stay, make their living, livelihood and indeed fortunes from this state. To expect them to learn the local language is not jingoism. It is the norm in most Indian states and cities. Why should Karnataka and Bangalore be any different?

Acknowledgements

Bangalore has been my home for nearly 20 years. It is a lovely city to live; a lovely home to raise children; and a welcoming haven for immigrants from all over the world.

This is my second book of essays about Bangalore. As always, it began with my column for *Hindustan Times.* For that, I have to thank R. Sukumar, the editor-in-chief, for not just suggesting the column but encouraging me to keep at it. At *HT Media,* I would also like to thank the folks who edited and copy-edited my work including Sheeba Manzoor, Ranu Joardar, Shilpa Ambardar, Vaibhav Sharma and many others.

Ever since I began writing for *HT Media,* beginning with *Mint Lounge*'s first issue in February 2007, Sukumar has been my editor and supporter. When I quit writing 'The Good Life' column for *Mint Lounge,* he moved me to *Hindustan Times* to write a column for *HT Brunch,* called 'This Indian Life'. During Covid, thanks to downsizing, that column was stopped. Sukumar then asked me to write a column about Bangalore. That is how this book began.

Dibakar Ghosh at Rupa saw the potential in this book, almost before I did. The team at Rupa were my earliest publishers in India. I am delighted to return to the fold with this book. My thanks to Dibakar for our conversations and his stewardship of the book; and to Padma Pegu who meticulously copy-edited this book and improved it greatly. Also to the marketing and publicity department, including Vasundhara Raj Baigra, Geetu Martolia and Priyanshi Sharma, who helped connect the book to its readers. Thanks also to the sales and accounting teams—Rita Satyawali, A.K. Singh, Rajen Das, Manjunath and everyone, especially in the Bangalore office—for ensuring that the book stayed current and stocked in bookstores.

Living and working in Bangalore has been a pleasure and a relief, given how welcoming this city is of immigrants like me. Most of the people who influenced my stay in Bangalore are already mentioned in this book. Here are a few other institutions who have enlivened our lives here: Takshashila Institution, Centre for Wildlife Studies (CWS), Natya Institute of Kathak & Choreography (NIKC), the Neev Literature Festival (NLF) and the Bangalore International Centre (BIC), and Sabha. They have helped me understand the many facets of the city.

Informal groups have also made this city immensely pleasurable. They include Author Evenings hosted in a private home, the Salon of Ideas which is a loose informal group of friends, Adda Ladies, The Wine Connoisseurs (TWC), Bangalore Wine Club (BWC), Koramangala Lunch Group (KLG) and the Crafts Council events.

Friends make a city into a home. In that, I am richly blessed. I have learned from and enjoyed the company of many Bangaloreans—too numerous to mention here. I would like to specifically mention a few people who are a great source of ideas for me. I call them frequently to bounce ideas through them. They include, in alphabetical order, Aliyeh Rizvi, Bala Mani, Chetan Kamani, Devesh Agarwal, Madhu Natraj, Marc Lamy, Naresh Narasimhan, Radhika Misra, Ramya Nagaraj, Shreedevi Deshpande Puri, Sree Gururaja, Suresh Jayaram, Udaya Kumar P.L, Ullas & Prathibha Karanth, V. Ravichander, and Yashodara Shroff, among others. I am grateful to them for their conversations and recommendations.

A special treat has been my intersection with nature. Bangalore is where I began birdwatching and it is how I developed rich friendships with many people including Mamlakatoi Hardikova, Priya Venkatesh, Karthikeyan S., Seshadri K.S., Vidisha Kulkarni, Sugandhi Gadadhar, Rana Belur, T.S. Srinivasa, M.B. Krishna, Deepa Mohan, Priya Singh, Shubha Bhat, L. Shyamal, S. Subramanya and many others.

The ideas in this book (as with all my books) were refined and enhanced through many rounds of brainstorming with my husband. He remains my catalyst, muse and enabler of projects. My daughters, Ranjini and Malini, are quickly going from children to my role-models. I am proud of who they have become. They grew up in Bangalore and every part of this city has memories for them. It is this gift that Bangalore has given our family.

My mother, Padma Narayanaswamy, and my mother-in-law, Padma Ramachandran, have blessed this book with success. I owe them a lot as I do my late father, V.R. Narayanaswamy, and father-in-law, V. Ramachandran.

My sister-in-law, Dr Lakshmi, and her husband, Dr Krishnan, have been nurturing presences in my life, as have their family. I hope to get them to spend more time with us in Namma Bangalore.

Part 1 of *Namma Bangalore* was dedicated to my brother and sister-in-law, Shyam and Priya Sunder. Together with their children, Sangeeta and Harsha, they were our first home in Bangalore. We stayed with them for close to two years when we first moved to India from Singapore. Later, we bought our own apartment in their building. They have been guides and beacons during our early years. Now, we have settled into a comfortable routine as neighbours and family. It is a thrill to enjoy this city with them.

Part 2 is dedicated to a friend who (like good friends do) opened up a new way of looking at the world, specifically nature. As someone who loves being in nature, I hope that I can do more of that in the coming years. I love the old Hindu idea of Vanaprastha, or going into the forests. But in order to do that, we need to preserve these forests and all the creatures that inhabit them. This heroine is attempting that, and for that, I dedicate this book to her.